Preparing the
Marketing Plan

AMERICAN MARKETING ASSOCIATION

NEW EDITION

Preparing the Marketing Plan

AMA MARKETING TOOLBOX

David Parmerlee

NTC Business Books

NTC/Contemporary Publishing Group

Library of Congress Cataloging-in-Publication Data

Parmerlee, David.
    Preparing the marketing plan / David Parmerlee.— New ed.
        p.   cm. — (American Marketing Association marketing toolbox)
    ISBN 0-658-00134-5
        1. Marketing—Management. 2. Strategic planning.   I. Title. II. Series.
    HF5415.13.P3248   2000
    658.8—dc21   99-52068
                                                            CIP

3 2280 00724 6135

Cover design by Nick Panos
Cover illustration copyright © Rob Colvin for Artville
Interior design by City Desktop Productions, Inc.

Published by NTC Business Books (in conjunction with the American
Marketing Association)
A division of NTC/Contemporary Publishing Group, Inc.
4255 West Touhy Avenue, Lincolnwood (Chicago), Illinois 60712-1975 U.S.A.
Copyright © 2000, 1993 by NTC/Contemporary Publishing Group
Printed in the United States of America
International Standard Book Number: 0-658-00134-5
00   01   02   03   04   05   VP   15   14   13   12   11   10   9   8   7   6   5   4   3   2   1

This book is dedicated to those I left behind.

Contents

Preface

Many marketing management books only define marketing and provide terminology definitions. The AMA Marketing Toolbox has a different purpose. This series will guide you in analyzing and articulating marketing data and applying it to real-world marketing actions. Although definitions are included, they are provided to form the basis for how to manage marketing effectively. The narrative aspects of these books describe the components of marketing processes. These books define the relationships between the processes and explain how they all work together. The books also supply sample formats (or templates) to help you create sophisticated marketing documents from your data.

A Systematic Process

Because markets change constantly and new marketing techniques appear all the time, a step-by-step system is needed to ensure accuracy. These books are process-based to allow you to be as thorough as possible in your marketing activities and document preparation. The books address marketing for the consumer package product, business-to-business or industrial manufacturing, and service industries.

For Marketers

Although these books are written with a "how-to" theme, they are written for marketers who have experience and who know marketing terminology and the objectives of the business function of marketing. The AMA Marketing Toolbox series consists of the following books:

- *Auditing Markets, Products, and Marketing Plans*
- *Developing Successful Marketing Strategies*
- *Preparing the Marketing Plan*

Role of the Marketing Plan

How does the marketing plan you will create using this book fit in with the other marketing processes? The marketing plan is the final step in this series. It determines and explains what, why, how, when, and where events and activities will happen. This annual plan tells you what to expect in the coming year, how you will deliver on your goals, and what it will cost. A marketing plan implements your strategies through tactics that sell your products at acceptable profit levels.

The books in the AMA Marketing Toolbox series will help you evaluate the markets and customers you serve, the products you offer, and methods by which those products are marketed to that marketplace. The following diagram indicates where each book fits into this process.

Research ⟶ Analysis ⟶ Planning

Data Sources:
Primary
Secondary   *Auditing Markets, Products,*   *Developing Successful*   *Preparing the*
Database   *and Marketing Plans*   *Marketing Strategies*   *Marketing Plan*
Internal

Introduction

What Is Marketing Management and Planning?

When one poses this question to various business executives, their replies are almost always broad or abstract. To further illustrate the various interpretations of this subject, ask ten business executives to describe how marketing as a business function contributes to their company's success and you will probably receive ten different answers.

The reason for this is because marketing suffers from an identity crisis like no other business function. Accounting, manufacturing, and human resources, for example, are all considered fairly well defined; marketing, on the other hand, is not. The reasons for this situation are so numerous it would take another book to explain it. Instead, this book addresses this facet of marketing management by defining the established standards.

To produce and implement a pure, balanced marketing plan, the term *marketing management* must be practiced and recognized by the organization and the customers it serves. As businesses struggle to better define what marketing is, they also need to devote their energies to defining how it should be organized around customers and products. Changes in technology, a diverse global economy, and sophisticated customers who are media savvy and demand more and more value are dictating that marketing management be a complete and strong aspect of a company's business practices. The marketing plan must reflect not only the action plan for a given year, it must represent an approach to marketing that is more than a glorified sales plan or media buying strategy. To survive and succeed in today's marketing landscape, companies must move from "power and control over" to "empowerment and cooperation of" marketing individuals. New methods such as sales automation, integrated marketing, process-based marketing organizations, and digital media access must be employed.

In defining marketing management from the concept of the word "marketing," marketing management is the *actual management of the process of developing marketing thoughts*. It is the ability to isolate, control, and program the function of marketing. If it were not for the function of marketing, the capitalist, or free enterprise, system would not exist as we know it. Thus marketing is the activity that creates a bridge between the item of value for sale and the customer who wants/needs that item.

What Are the Origins of Marketing Management and Planning?

Marketing gets its roots from economics. During the 1890s and perhaps earlier, students in economics at the great German business schools often went to time-consuming lengths to study firsthand the market forces in various economies. As a result, it became apparent that some type of activity had to be developed to collect data and analyze them in such a manner that the results would be scientifically accurate. Marketing was born.

By the early 1900s, many American students who had studied in Europe returned to the United States to become professors. In the process of designing courses for teaching business principles, marketing was included as part of the curriculum. Based on what they had experienced, the professors believed that marketing courses were keys to the core education that included administration, accounting, and finance. The conditions that existed during this time were less complex than those of today. Back then, markets were likely to be local or regional in their geographic scope. Communicating with people took days or even weeks. The workforce was primarily unskilled and uneducated and performed manual labor. The economy had less fluctuation and experienced slow, if any, change. The need for a marketing function was minimal.

In 1906, a University of Wisconsin professor, Samuel Sparling, published *Introduction to Business Organization* (New York: Macmillan, 1906). In this publication, early marketing and its organizational principles began to take shape. It discussed only one discipline, research, but began to discuss the functions of a total marketing approach (Exhibit 1). Because business of that era was heavy manufacturing, the functions presented focused primarily on the act of distribution and its ability to facilitate exchange. However, in one section of this book, Sparling included chapters that talked about the evolution of market dynamics, direct selling and salesmanship, wholesaling and retailing, mail-order business, advertising credits, and collections. Sparling definitely saw marketing as a main element of the science of business.

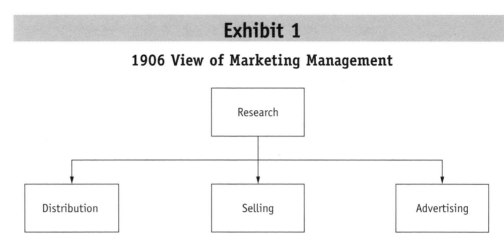

Exhibit 1

1906 View of Marketing Management

Research

Distribution   Selling   Advertising

The type of management organizational structure used at this time in marketing was the standard hierarchical system, born from the military and churches. This system limited the amount of decision making any one marketing person could do; it provided the top manager/supervisor close control over his or her employees, and customers had little voice. Information was guarded and not openly shared and, as a result, communications and idea exchange were very limited.

As the decades came and went, marketing began to expand its role. Marketing management was viewed primarily as a research tool for business, and therefore marketing plans were narrow and almost clinical. Although research was the dominant component to marketing management, other areas began to grow. The other two marketing disciplines besides research—analysis and planning—began establishing their value and identities. Obviously, data collected had to be translated into an action plan and, as part of that plan, the functional areas (distribution, selling, advertising, etc.) began their own development. From the earlier, simple form, marketing began to be known by the famous "four Ps concept," which stood for product, place, price, and promotion.

Like everything else in business management, old definitions and standard functionality began to shift because of changing markets. These markets were forcing businesses to modernize and again become more sophisticated in how they approached marketing. As technology changed (e.g., the advent of radio and broadcast television), marketing took on more importance. Customers' buying behavior was becoming increasingly difficult to predict. In addition, reaching them with a message that would call them to action (buying or influencing the buying) was equally becoming more complex to deliver.

By the 1960s and 1970s, when American society experienced great social revolutions, emphasis on all elements of marketing took flight. As the old structure of the marketing department's resources was being stretched, a new sophisticated structure had to be devised. Businesses expanded marketing's role by creating new methods (e.g., event and sales promotions), increasing the number of marketing management executives controlling projects and tasks, and expanding their responsibilities.

Philip Kotler, one of the world's leading authorities and professor of marketing at Northwestern University, published *Marketing Management: Analysis, Planning, and Control* (Englewood Cliffs, NJ: Prentice Hall, 1967). This book became the standard for graduate students and established marketing as more than just a sales function. Kotler demonstrated that marketing had become a complex group of functions (advertising, product management, etc.) and that time needed to be spent on the formation of a marketing organization to run this group of functions. He determined that the marketing management element of business not only needed to exist, but could exist in different versions of a business's pattern of evolution. He established five separate versions, or stages, of marketing management and evolutionary paths of development. These stages (modified to reflect the planning aspect) are as follows (in order of evolution):

1. Simple sales plan

2. Sales and marketing plan

3. Separate marketing plan

4. Modern marketing plan (integrated marketing functions)

5. Modern marketing company (integrating marketing with other business functions)

During this time frame, product managers became the driving force within marketing management. A product plan (offering the best products and/or introducing new products to the product line) became a key component of the marketing plan. Although the focus was still on the overall management of marketing, the product manager, especially in the consumer package product markets (also known as the "brand manager"), took on the responsibility of integrating each available marketing function into the product designation plan.

After the recession of the early 1980s, marketing management changed again. Big marketing budgets and resources were cut to reduce operating expenses. Business expected more from less, and the need for marketing productivity and efficiency was the mantra of the day. Customer satisfaction and customer relationship building became for some companies the lifeline to merely exist. Marketing planning, as a result, began to be driven by product delivery and customer service. Market management, especially customer management, became equally or more important as the products being marketed. Marketing planning began to focus on market plans. Like the product plan focus, market plans (how to define and target the marketplace) took on a key role in the marketing plan. Therefore the marketing plan focused on matching products to customers by type definitions and then matching marketing activities to points where those two elements intersected.

With the advent of personal computers in the middle to late 1980s, every marketer had technology at his or her desk. Target and micromarketing and information management came into vogue as a result. This gave marketing quick access to information and allowed for faster delivery of goods and services. For the first time, a marketing manager in a medium to small company could manage marketing like the big Madison Avenue companies. Businesses valued a real marketing management approach because marketing had the information and the technology to cost-effectively market products to customers, which had a direct impact on profit.

As the 1990s began to unfold, American corporations looked to marketing as a business tool. They saw it as a business function that worked with customer service, product distribution, and finance/accounting to meet flow-of-business challenges. Marketing plans reflected this trend by linking sales and profitability forecasts to the company's pro forma statements (income, cash flow, and the balance sheet). Companies also realized that if they teamed marketing with these other departments then communications problems (about generating revenues and/or getting the most of budget dollars, for example) between the departments would be lessened. Marketing plans were integrating all functions of marketing. A marketing plan was a balanced blend of research (product and market), product development/management and pricing, communications (advertising, promotions, and public relations), and sales and selling. Like the market and product plans that drive the direction of a marketing plan, individual marketing functions had their own plans. Advertising, sales management and selling, pricing, and so on had plans that were specific but integrated into the total marketing plan (Exhibit 2).

Exhibit 2

The Nine Marketing Functions

Where Is Marketing Management and Planning Today?

Conditions today are more complex than they were one hundred years ago. Markets are now global in their geographic scope. Communicating with people is instantaneous. The modern-day workforce is skilled and well educated and works with computers and robots. With the focus on the stock market, the pressure for companies to have a high annual return on investment, and an unpredictable global economy, the marketplace can experience rapid changes almost daily. Mass marketing is no more and micromarketing, propounding one-to-one relationships with customers, is here to stay. The need for an integrated, flexible, and technology-dependent marketing plan is not a luxury—it is essential.

As businesses move into the twenty-first century, the famous four Ps concept could now almost stand for probing, partitioning, prioritizing, and positioning. The demands placed on a company to survive and succeed in the marketplace are being transferred directly to the marketing plan and the marketing department/organization. Marketing has become a lightning rod for information processing about internal performance (sales, revenue, etc.) and external market activity and/or demand measurement (market potential, customer buying trends, etc.). Exhibit 3 shows the "new" marketing thinking.

Exhibit 3

The New Marketing Thinking

What's Out	What's In
Size	Speed
Stability	Change
Hierarchy	Business development teams
Mere customer service	Customer-driven processes
Organization around functions	Organization around products
Marketing managers	Marketing leaders/coaches
Worker bees	Workers trained, empowered, and held responsible

Marketing planning today still uses the core principles that have been successful and popular for the last twenty years. What is new is the technology and the manner in which those principles are applied. The marketing plan structure provided in this book addresses marketing from a detailed and integrated viewpoint. It has been designed to produce as an end result a document that acts as a blueprint to follow in implementing a business's tactics and overall strategies for one year. Although the process features a structured format, it is flexible and open to change if internal or external forces dictate.

To understand how beliefs in marketing management and planning are changing, you merely need to look at the landscape of the marketing industry. Ten years ago, if you asked someone to name the top companies that practiced sophisticated marketing and the management thereof, names such as Procter & Gamble, Kraft General Foods, Colgate-Palmolive, Lever Brothers, or Quaker would most likely have been the response. A person would have given these names because of their traditional stature in the marketplace. This was due to their level of product/brand management, product and market research, and advertising spending expertise. Everyone in the marketing world always wanted to emulate them in shaping a company/marketing department for a successful run.

Today, however, if you ask marketing experts who they watch regarding marketing changes, they would not say those companies. In fact, they most likely would tell you those old marketing organizations have been replaced by new leaders such as MCI, Sprint, Hewlett-Packard, Amazon.com, American Express, L.L. Bean, or JCPenney. These organizations have taken the lead because they have done away with traditional marketing concepts and approaches that have been used since the 1950s.

Marketing plans in the past depended on mass marketing as their overriding approach. Those earlier, "sophisticated" organizations have maintained this approach, even with their markets becoming more and more fragmented. This old marketing planning thinking can be described as "inside-out." This means companies/marketing departments tend to first establish what type of goal they would like to achieve (e.g., level of sales or profits). They then set out to find customers (suspects to prospects) who will allow them to reach those goals. As a result, their marketing plans always tend to be playing catch-up.

A comparison between how the old lions use marketing and the approach the new marketing leaders are taking is outlined in Exhibit 4. In this example, you can see how marketing is changing and how companies/marketing departments are changing how they configure their marketing plans. The companies/marketing departments that would be considered the sophisticates of the marketing world today tend to use the approach called "outside-in." This means instead of first focusing on establishing goals, they focus on customers' or potential customers' needs. To do this, the new marketing planning takes into account the customer database, with the focus on customer satisfaction and retention. Instead of spending time trying to only predict customer demand and/or level of buying power/activity, they focus on what the customer wants. This approach is commonly known as *integrated marketing*, or essentially outside-in marketing.

Exhibit 4

Characteristics of Marketers Using
Inside-Out and Outside-In Marketing

Inside-Out Marketing	Outside-In Marketing
Approach	
• Know little about their customers • Think of markets, not people • Rely on traditional survey research to tell them the "average consumer" • Look at marketing in "averages"	• Think of the customer/prospect as number one • Define customers by using longitudinal data, rational databases, perceptual modeling, and scoring of customers to determine what they like/might like in the future
Focus	
• Concentrate on customer conquest • Constantly thinking about new customers, taking business from the competition, and extending the product line to bring in new customers • Think in terms of the short term, don't care who buys or what it costs to produce a sale, as long as it gets them business	• Rely on relationship building with their customers • Concentrate on customer satisfaction by keeping each customer so happy that they become the organization's advocate in the marketplace (e.g., Lexus or Saturn car owners)
Goal Orientation	
• Care only about making the numbers (market share, sales volume, etc.) • Risk the future to meet internal goals by mortgaging the organization's key assets	• Place high value on keeping customers over a long period of time • Create income flow systems to track cost per customer sale to know how much to spend to get a new one and better understand their true cost of marketing • Focus on customer qualification and prioritizing to determine the most profitable and accessible to sell to
Management Style	
• Driven by efficiency, they take a cut-and-slash approach to fixing problems, regardless of the ultimate outcome • Use mass marketing no matter what	• Driven by how effective they are, not how efficient • Work to be a "low-cost marketer," not a "low-cost producer"

Source: Adapted and modified from Don E. Schultz's column on integrated marketing organizations from "Marketing News," June 6, 1994.

Integrated marketing takes the nine marketing functions (shown in Exhibit 2) and places them on an equal playing field. This allows marketing to take a truly integrated approach that is not slanted toward one function or another. For example, typically the sales function (department) tends to get favored status because many or most of the revenue generated by a company comes from the "transaction of the sale." But if sales were to run the marketing plan, the plan would cater to sales demands such as pricing or product development, which could produce risky or unprofitable results. It also takes the communication portion (advertising, promotions, and public relations) and links it with the remaining functions to generate information in a manner that complements each function in perfect harmony. Thus, a marketing plan focuses on all marketing functions, instead of just one or two.

Marketing management is changing its thinking so it can quickly respond to market demand by accelerating new product introduction. It is responding by being more active in changing product mix, placing and maneuvering orders through the system faster, and distributing/delivering products at a far greater pace. It is focusing on product innovation and arranging marketing organization around processes, not functions.

The new marketing plan relies heavily on the element of customer satisfaction measurement (CSM), which relates to service and support. It has become the defining symbol in marketing management today. In the mid-1980s, customer satisfaction measurement was used as a tool with total quality management (TQM) and quality assurance programs to ensure high levels of product/service quality and customer happiness. Although it was used to help shape customer response/support, most marketers thought of it as a good public opinion or public relations move to keep their customers loyal.

Throughout this period, however, marketers realized that customer happiness represented more than just positive reinforcement. They discovered that customers (current, potential, and former) were a source for business. This business would take the form of either add-on sales or entirely new sales. In fact, customers were a great source of new product/service ideas. The term "the Rs" was coined to define CSM as the following:

- Recruit new customers

- Retain existing customers

- Regain lost customers

If you look at integrated marketing and customer satisfaction measurement concepts together as a total approach, you might describe it as micromarketing. This approach can define not only both of these concepts, but the state of marketing management in terms of the new direction in its thinking. In today's fractured world, companies/marketing departments are finding novel ways to reach elusive customers.

Basically, micromarketing is customer servicing with high-tech marketing technology, which uses market processes and point-of-sale positioning tactics to define, identify, reach, obtain, and/or retain customers. Although this approach is primarily directed at the consumer package product industry (suppliers and retailers), its principles can be applied to the industrial manufacturing, business-to-business, and service-oriented industries as well. In 1988, Stan Rapp and Tom Collins wrote the book *MaxiMarketing* (New York: McGraw-Hill, 1988), which addressed the "future shock type" situation that existed in marketing and outlined where it was going in the future. This book discussed many of the same elements that make up micromarketing; as a result, many marketers consider the terms to be interchangeable.

Micro-, or maxi-, marketing technology identifies individuals by "data mapping," or using consumption patterns of where they live or work (marketing Geographic Information Systems, or GIS, program). This allows a marketer to perform functions such as customer profiling, market size analysis, and site selection/analysis, as well as all other marketing functions and activities. Database marketing is the key tool marketers rely on to market their products/services in this micro/maxi world.

Working as a key component of integrated marketing, this process starts and ends with data comprising collected information about customers/prospects. Marketing programs tailored for those customers are implemented with the results from programs fed back into the database for another round of data manipulation.

Going back to our original question: What is marketing management and planning? The marketing plan is an annual plan of how you are going to market your products or services in the marketplace. It is the end result of your efforts of analyzing and isolating the problems and opportunities associated with your marketplace, customer base, product offerings, and management of marketing. It is the next step of your strategic marketing plan and the framework in which your marketing actions are formed to meet and exceed your expectations.

How Should This Book Be Used?

This book provides you with a set of marketing planning formats to help you prepare a document in which your marketing plan can be presented in an organized fashion. The processes and formats in this book contain examples that reflect a consumer package goods orientation. When industry-specific differences exist, separate formats are used or the differences noted. The size and complexity of your company may also require adjustments.

Preparing to Build Your Marketing Plan

The first six units in this book are designed to lead you through a step-by-step process. This includes organizing information about your company, products, and marketing objectives and activities in order to create a marketing plan document. The seventh unit provides insight regarding the best approach to preparing, presenting, and activating your marketing plan.

Marketing Thinking

Before using the formats in this book, you will need to have audited and analyzed data relevant to your particular marketing operation. To increase the effectiveness of this book, you should have completed the other two books in the series (*Auditing Markets, Products, and Marketing Plans* and *Developing Successful Marketing Strategies*). Those books address the steps that ideally should be performed to properly build and manage your marketing plan efforts.

Marketing Planning

The formats in this book will help you use the data collected to create a clear, understandable document to direct and shape your marketing efforts. Each unit measures factors that impact your marketing activities. By following the step-by-step process in these seven units, you will have a clear annual plan and budget for carrying out your marketing tactical plans.

The Marketing Plan

To this point, we have discussed the purpose of a marketing plan and how marketing management and planning has evolved through the years to become the cornerstone of business it is today. This book provides the structure and the elements that can be used to build a marketing plan document. Before we begin assembling your thoughts about piecing together your marketing puzzle, you need to understand the process and pitfalls of marketing plan creation.

The Modern Marketing Plan

In the past, the common basis for constructing a marketing plan and the thought process behind that plan was built on standardization. Successful marketing planning relied heavily on standardizing products and the communication about and distribution of those products—and, in the process, the standardization of the customer. The entire premise of sophisticated marketing was to segment customers and match them to the products the company was offering. This was a cost-effective method of defining, selecting, reaching, and capturing the customer. Even those companies that offered products originating from a targeted group of customers still viewed those customers as cattle, herding them to the market.

Although the standardized approach still has some merit, it is quickly being replaced by what is being coined as a "one-to-one" approach. This blends the sophistication of the process marketing game that standardized everything with more of a customization through products and marketing actions. Instead of focusing on one product at a time and attempting to market it to as many "like" customer segments as possible, marketing plans need to concentrate on one customer at a time and selling that customer as many products as possible over the customer's lifetime. This is known as *relationship marketing,* or *customer life cycle marketing.*

Life Cycle Management

Throughout this book, especially in Unit 3 where the marketing mix functions are programmed, the life cycles are discussed. The following life cycle models are cited often:

- Customer life cycle

- Market life cycle

- Product life cycle

These three models are used to drive how a marketing department should be developing its strategies and tactics. Each model is based on the concept that life flows in stages. In the case of the market and product models, they experience the same four stages of life: introduction, growth, maturity, and decline.

Each stage presents a product or market with a different set of variables that, on average, will occur. As a result, you can look at the market you are in or considering entering and determine the degree of life that remains. With products, you can assess your current products (as well as those of your competitors) to determine how much longer those products (using the current formulas or configuration) can compete. The customer model conceptually works in the same manner, but the stages are different. A customer's life cycle will depend on his or her relationship with you. Although customers will grow, mature, and die, their life cycles tend to focus on life-changing events.

Many books are available on the subject of life cycle marketing. They can provide you with common objectives, strategies, and tactics. They also can offer characteristics such as sales, costs, profits, and customer and competitor behavior. All of this information is provided, based, and categorized along the stages of a given life cycle. This will help you shape the framework of your marketing plan.

The Customer and the Marketing Plan

Customer databases, life cycle modeling, and customer behavior tracking must all be used in building your marketing plan. Although each dynamic of a marketplace (competition, customers, etc.) is important, customers are the obvious key.

The customer tends to be viewed only as new, additional customers or new types of customers. That is still true, but it needs to be augmented by looking to current and former customers as part of the overall customer base or segmentation. Thus your marketing plan (market/customer plan) needs to focus on being able to gather specific information about your customers and then on retaining and reselling to current customers, as well as reaching new customers.

Your marketing plans should also address technology. Technologies available to marketers today assist them in gaining knowledge about their customers and in establishing interactive communications with them. For example, the power of the Internet allows for customers to gain information and/or make a purchase. It can provide your company with the ability to update sales volume or on-line inventory changes. This is an example of automated marketing.

This book is based on process marketing, which means processes to build and follow in creating a marketing plan. It blends stable growth and low-risk tactics with new technologies that manage your customers and products.

Your marketing plan must reflect the economic business realities of an annual rate of return on investment (ROI). This means your marketing ideas must be reached and returned in the current year, regardless of next year's prospects.

Other key points to remember are integrating your marketing ideas with establishing ownership, milestones, measurement/renewal and alignment with strategies, tactics, and specific actions. In addition to the customer, your marketing plan should focus on the marketing organization and how it relates to the rest of your company. It should be linked directly to revenues and expense performance. Management issues must be identified and resolutions must be included.

Presenting and Assembling Your Marketing Plan

No matter what is new and what is old with marketing management today, the bottom line is still the same: Your marketing strategies and tactics must either make your company more money than last year (income generation) and/or save your company money compared with last year (cost control).

Note: The order in which the elements of your marketing plan are developed will be different than the order in which they will appear in the final document. The reason for this is that a marketing plan must tell a story in a manner readers want to read. Therefore, sales and revenue forecasts are always number one, because those data drive the company for the year. Exhibit 5 profiles how you will build the elements of your plan (step by step) and then assemble those elements in an order that tells the story of marketing you wish to present.

Exhibit 5

Order of Steps to Build a Marketing Plan

	Order of Events	
	Presentation View	**Assembling View**
Marketing Achievements		
Marketing objectives summary	1	29
Sales and revenue forecasting	2	8
Product profitability projections	3	9
Market size estimating	4	4
Market share assessment	5	10
Business expansion and growth goals	6	5
Marketing organizational structure	7	24
Marketing information systems	8	11
Strategic Direction		
Overall marketing management strategic plan	9	1
Market strategy	10	2
Product strategy	11	3
Programming		
Overall marketing management tactical plan	12	28
Research and data management plan	13	16
Product management and development plan	14	6
Pricing plan	15	7
Distribution plan	16	13
Sales management and selling plan	17	12
Advertising plan	18	14
Promotions plan	19	15
Public relations plan	20	17
Legal marketing plan	21	18
Implementation		
Scheduling the marketing mix	22	19
Media placement selection	23	20
Budgeting		
Overall marketing mix expenses	24	21
Individual marketing mix expenses	25	22*
Market/customer to product line expenses	26	23
Controls		
Reporting and tracking	27	25
Corrective actions and managing change	28	26
Updating and planning for next year	29	27

*Once this element is completed, company cost limits may dictate an adjustment back through the prior twenty-one elements to make the budget work in the manner required.

Preparing the Marketing Plan

DATA ANALYSIS

The seven units in this book are designed to lead you through a step-by-step process of organizing information about your company, products, and marketing objectives and activities in order to create a marketing plan document. Before using the formats in this book, you will need to have collected, processed, tabulated, and analyzed data relevant to your particular marketing operation. The formats in the book will help you use that data to create a clear, understandable document to direct and shape your marketing efforts.

Each unit measures factors that impact your marketing activities. By following the step-by-step process in these seven units, you will have a clear annual plan and budget for carrying out your marketing tactics in each marketing function area, all substantiated with hard data in a document that will give you confidence as a marketing decision maker.

Predicting Your Marketing Achievements

The marketing plan document comprises six units. These units departmentalize your plan into the elements that drive what, when, why, where, how, and by whom marketing efforts will be carried out during the coming year. Each unit serves a specific purpose for the reader or user of the information contained in the plan.

The first unit profiles the vital signs for your plan and marketing actions. It measures the expected outcomes of your marketing efforts and provides insight as to how your plan will deliver on your goals.

Your marketing plan begins with the following items:

- Cover page

- Contact list (with telephone numbers and E-mail addresses)

- Table of contents (items and page numbers)

- Methodology (how you arrived at your conclusions and recommendations, if needed)

- Executive summary (marketing objectives)

- Marketing achievements (expectations for the coming year)

- Strategic direction

- Programming

- Implementation

- Budgeting

- Controls

Your executive summary can be part of your marketing achievements section or used as a lead-in or introduction to this section—it is your decision.

Marketing Objectives Summary

Like most business documents, your marketing plan should begin with an executive summary. This summary encapsulates the contents of the marketing plan to give the reader an overview of your goals and objectives and what to expect for the coming year. The summary should be prepared at the end of your marketing planning process. In your summary, you must identify the key performance indicators (KPIs) related to anticipated growth rates and performance levels in terms of increasing dollars, units, and percentages.

Key Performance Indicators

Your summary should be based on your long-term strategic marketing plan and short-term tactical outlook. These goals and objectives are rooted in vision, such as image or position in the industry, but they almost always need to be connected to one or more of the standard data points:

- Sales volume generation

- Financial return or return on investment (ROI)

- Marketing cost control

- Market share direction

- Overall growth (sales, revenues, or income)

    Your executive summary should include the following elements:

- Needs, problems, and opportunities facing the company in the coming year

- The current marketplace conditions and predicted changes

- Goals and objectives

- Strategies, including major recommendations and principal action programs

- Marketing tactics and actions (overview form)

Writing the Summary

The executive summary is where you make your case about what you want to achieve and why. You must express your ideas in a fashion that excites the senior management of the company and stimulates interest in your marketing team.

This section must convey your goals in narrative statements that integrate the numbers that drive your business. This balancing act is important because many staff members will learn of your marketing plans only through this document. Remember, the purpose of this section is to use text to polish the KPI numbers and present an overview of the plan's vital signs, which will ultimately be the measurement of your marketing plan's success.

If appropriate, it may be important to incorporate your company's corporate or business division marketing goals and objectives into those of your marketing department. Each objective must reflect the needs of both the company and the marketing department.

Sales and Revenue Forecasting

After you have established your marketing goals, it's time to start setting numerical objectives. This is the cornerstone of your marketing plan. It is one of your most important tasks, not only for your marketing area, but for your entire company. Your sales and revenue forecasts establish a pipeline for the inflow of business or commerce into your company and drive your company's operations for the coming year.

The Basis for Estimates

You must establish a formula on which to base all of your estimates, predictions, projections, and forecasts. To do this, you may use the following factors, derived from your prior market, product, and marketing management audits:

- Market potential (from your market size model)

- Market forecast (from your market size model)

- Production capacity

- Sales potential (from your market size model)

- Market trends

- Market financial health (market attractiveness)

- Product profitability

- Marketing activities (distribution/service area)

Once you have obtained the data from these factors, you need to begin plugging them into your annual forecast. You must be as objective as possible to ensure the accuracy and the validity of the forecast. Ask yourself the following questions:

Quantitative Verification

- Are your data time specific?

- Are your data measurable?

- Can you track your data by product, customer, sales, territory, and distributor sources?

Qualitative Verification

- Are your data realistic?

- Are your accounting methods sound?

- Do your data reflect seasonal fluctuations?

- Do your numbers reflect sound financial results?

Building and Displaying Your Forecasts

To create the structure that will house your sales forecasts, Formats 1 and 2 provide you with a sample format. The first format summarizes year-end sales volume predictions. The second format is a breakout of the year by individual months. It is good practice to forecast sales and revenue goals on a monthly basis for the upcoming year and then quarterly for the following two years, if you so desire. This allows you to show how sales fluctuations that occur throughout the year impact your sales flow and to make sure you obtain the important year-end totals. Complete both formats by defining your percentage of sales volume contribution, sales in dollar volume, corresponding units sold, and growth rate from the previous year.

Format 1				
One-Year Summary of Sales Forecasts				
Product	**Sales Volume (%)**	**$**	**Units**	**Annual Growth (%)**
ABC	75	150,000	500	7
ABC2	25	50,000	500	5
Total	100	200,000	1,000	6

Format 2

Sales Forecasts for One Year, by Month

Product	Jan $	Jan Units	Feb $	Feb Units	Mar $	Mar Units
ABC	1,000	50	4,000	80	10,000	150
ABC2	800	30	2,000	50	5,000	80
Total	1,800	80	6,000	130	15,000	230

The terms "sales" and "revenue" can mean the same thing or different things, depending on your definition. The difference between sales and revenue is the allowances for loss, returns, or discounts. If your intent is to consider sales and revenue forecasts as one and the same, you must identify them as "net" sales generated after allowances. If your company wants to show sales separate from revenue forecasts, you need to apply the following formula and show results using a format similar to that for the sales forecast.

Unit volume – Allowance (average) $\times$ Price (per unit average) = Revenue

It should be noted that when product sales volumes are totaled together, averages may be used to reach a total. The pricing plan section goes into greater detail regarding revenues and their relationship to sales.

Summarizing Your Annual Sales Forecasts

In addition to quantitative display, you should state your sales and revenue forecasts in narrative form, as in the following examples:

- "Increase specific product sales by 5 percent during the next fiscal year."

- "Increase the number of customers by 15 percent by the end of the fiscal year."

- "Increase sales volume by 30 percent in selected target markets or sales territories by specific dates."

This can tie back to the previous goals and objectives in the opening section.

Product Profitability Projections

Everything you do in business, especially in marketing, should be judged by its impact on the bottom line. The purpose of establishing profitability projections is to determine the revenues that will be generated as a result of your sales activity. Your product profitability statement will include pricing (which you will determine in the pricing plan section) and product costs (which you will determine with the help of your accountant or financial manager).

You should break down your profitability projections by individual product and overall product line using Format 3. The information in this format also will enable you to link your sales forecasts with pricing structure.

Format 3	
Product Profitability Projections	
20____	
Overall	
Sales in Dollars	200,000
Sales in Units	1,000
Rate of Growth (%)	6.0
Cost of Goods Sold	100,000
Gross Profit	100,000
Gross Margin (%)	50.0
20____	
Product:	
Sales in Dollars	
Sales in Units	
Rate of Growth (%)	
Cost of Goods Sold	
Gross Profit	
Gross Margin (%)	

Basis for Estimates

Work with your controller/accountant to determine your pricing structure and cost of goods sold. These form the basis of your financial projections.

Each year you want to make more money to cover rising costs or to reinvest in the company; you do this by lowering costs, selling more product, or raising the product's price.

Alternative Income Sources

More and more companies are augmenting their traditional income (products or services) by establishing other sources of income. This is especially true in the service sector where financial institutions are looking to fee income to assist product income. If this is the case in your situation, you need to isolate the additional income and understand its implications. This includes how it will be profiled and tracked in sales, revenue, and profit models. Typically, additional income is reported separately from product and service business.

Market Size Estimating

The purpose of attempting to predict market size is to decide how you fit into that market as a result of your marketing actions (advertising, pricing, etc.). The market you are measuring must already have been defined during your market audit when market segmentation was performed. The market size is defined in terms of its parameters or limits and can reflect your universe, segment, or target market (customer groups). To complete this exercise, you must already know and be able to identify it by name (e.g., the "U.S. Home Consumer/Retail Electronics Market").

Defining Market Size

The market size is defined at four levels; the first two levels define the market and the second two define your capability of selling in the market. Level one is the market potential; its purpose is to establish the maximum possible dollar or unit sales of a product category for all firms within a defined area and period of time. It is the broadest description of market size. Market potential is key because it establishes your baseline for the other three levels and drives market penetration and share calculations. Thus, you need to take time to truly understand how big your market is.

Level two is the market forecast; its purpose is to establish the estimated actual dollar or unit sales of a product category for all firms (including your own) within the defined area and period of time. Market potential refers to the amount that *could* be sold; the market forecast establishes what *should* be sold.

To calculate the market forecast, add up all firms' year-end sales for the product category. If you have performed a market analysis, you will have this information available.

Level three is the sales potential; its purpose is to establish the maximum possible dollar or unit sales amount of product your company is capable of producing, selling, and servicing annually. This is based primarily on your ability to produce the product and to sell, distribute, and service customers for the year.

Level four is the sales forecast; its purpose is to predict estimated dollar or unit sales of your product line for the year. The sales forecast comes from the sales and revenue forecasts you established in the previous section.

You should develop market size models for your total market area, as well as for each target market. Break your estimates down by product to show each product's profitability.

Format 4 provides you with a method of displaying your estimated market size for the coming year. The overall figures reflect totals. The annual rate of growth overall is an average.

Market Share Assessment

Market share is a measurement of how your sales performance impacts the marketplace. It is the end result of your sales performance as it relates to the competition and the total market. The purpose of market share is to project what your "piece of the pie" will be in the coming year. This information will help direct your marketing mix planning.

Often you will be asked, "What is your market penetration?" *Market penetration* is a form of market share. It is used to identify how much of the market remains for growth. This is important because when your growth comes from a particular market, it will come from either your competitors or the available market.

Many times in presenting your marketing plan, the market saturation point will be required. This data point establishes where the end of the market is located. This is shown in sales by time (year) and by product. Thus, you can demonstrate (assuming current conditions remain constant) the remaining growth potential related to your market share.

Interpreting Market Share

Market share, like all the tools used in estimating your performance, is displayed by individual products and total product line. This is particularly helpful in market share because each product is marketed to a specific customer type (profile and status). A customer profile (shared attributes of customers who form a group) is used in finely tuning market segments and target markets. Customer status (the relationship with your company of a new, current, or former

Format 4

Market Size Model

20_____	$	Units	Annual Growth (%)
Market Potential			
Overall	10,000,000	100,000	2
Product: ABC	6,000,000	60,000	2
Product: ABC2	4,000,000	40,000	2
Market Forecast			
Overall	1,000,000	10,000	4
Product: ABC	600,000	6,000	5
Product: ABC2	400,000	4,000	3
Sales Potential			
Overall	500,000	5,000	3
Product: ABC	300,000	2,500	4
Product: ABC2	200,000	2,500	2
Sales Forecast			
Overall	200,000	1,000	6
Product: ABC	150,000	500	7
Product: ABC2	50,000	500	5

customer) defines the value of customers as they relate to marketing efforts. Showing market share by product references customer types to reflect new sales to new customers, new sales to current customers, and/or resales to current or former customers. Therefore, your market share percentage totals will include sales by product and customers compared with those of the competition.

Calculating Market Share

Market share also ranks you against your peers. Market share is usually shown as a two-digit percentage (e.g., 25 percent), whereas market penetration is hopefully shown in single digits (e.g., 3 percent)—low single digits mean higher market growth availability. Be sure to include the basis of your market estimates and the predicted direction and speed of market share growth or decline (yours and your competitors').

To determine market share for individual products, divide the market forecast or market potential by the annual sales forecast for the product.

$$\text{Market share relative to competition} = \frac{\text{Year-end sales forecast}}{\text{Market forecast}} = \frac{50,000}{100,000} = 50\%$$

$$\text{Market share relative to competition} = \frac{\text{Year-end sales forecast}}{\text{Market potential}} = \frac{50,000}{1,000,000} = 5\%$$

Format 5 provides a method of presenting your market share estimates.

Format 5

Market Share

20____	Market Share (Units)	Annual Growth (%)
Overall	10.0	6.0
Product: ABC	5.0	7.0
Product: ABC2	5.0	5.0

Business Expansion and Growth Goals

Very few businesses can function without formal activities designed to create growth. Most companies are constantly searching for avenues to pursue to expand their product line or increase their number of customers. Marketing plays a key role in this area, setting expansion objectives for both the company as a whole and marketing management. This is called a *growth strategy*. You can achieve growth through internal or external means.

Internal Goals

Growth through internal means is good, provided you have the proper resources and support. Growing by using your current base means more control and more income, but it also can mean more risk. You can select one or a combination of the following tactics to establishing growth:

- Add new customers with current products
- Add new products with current customers

- Add new customers with new products

- Combine any or all of these and/or expand market area

Exhibit 1-1 frames the options you have available in selecting your internal growth actions. You can address marketing from all the high-tech angles, but this exhibit gets down to the basics. Your product/market/customer mix comes from one or a combination of these options; for example, selling new product to current customers and former customers (available through your database).

Internal growth means you are growing purely on your ability to manage current and new products within (geographically defined) current and new markets and with current, new, and/or former customers. In short, you are simply going out to the market and bringing back more business.

Exhibit 1-1

Product/Market and Customer Options

(Mix and Select)

Product	Market	Customer
Current	Current	New Customer (Actual)
		Current Customer (Actual)
		Former Customer (Actual)
New	New	New Customer (Type)
		Current Customer (Type)
		Former Customer (Type)

External Goals

Growth through external means is also good, provided your sources have the proper resources and support. Growing by using someone else's resources means shared control and shared income; but it also means shared risk. In today's business world, very few companies are big enough to have total control over their own resources. You can select one or more of the following external growth tactics:

Acquisition

- Define new products you want

- Identify competitors who have those products

- Determine how you will acquire those products from the competitors
- Predict results of cost/revenue activities

Franchising

- Define geographic areas
- Identify type of franchising system and franchisers
- Develop franchisee plan
- Predict results of cost/revenue activities

Licensing

- Define what products could be licensed and to what degree
- Identify who wants licensing rights
- Develop contract/royalty arrangements for licensed products
- Predict results of cost/revenue activities

Business Relationship Alignment

- Define type of relationship (e.g., joint venture)
- Identify businesses for alignment
- Develop guidelines for relationship
- Predict results of cost/revenue activities

Your growth goals, internal and/or external, will be displayed in narrative form in your marketing plan. If growth percentages or sales volume increases (linked to growth tactics) are needed, you have the freedom to provide whatever data you need to convey the reasoning behind your plans.

Marketing Organizational Structure

The purpose of this section is to establish your plans for preparing your marketing team to deliver on the identified marketing goals. This preparation consists of improving your marketing staff's skills, expanding or reallocating your marketing staff, or altering the structure in which your marketing management efforts operate.

Your goal is to determine what, if any, changes will be made to your marketing department. You need to consider whether to expand or decrease your staff levels or to redesign your staff's job responsibilities. Then you need to address the costs of or savings from those changes. Costs such as training will fall under your departmental budget, whereas compensation packages fall under human relations or operations department budgets.

In the sales management plan, there is a section that focuses on outside sales force staffing needs. In the marketing plan, this section deals with your marketing management operational staff, support staff, functional area staff, and internal sales staff. This section is usually shown in narrative form with an organization flow chart.

In your marketing management audit, you determined and selected the changes needed to form your marketing team. This included the structural and cultural changes needed to reorganize how your marketing department works and how it relates to other departments in the company.

Structural and Cultural Considerations

If you have decided to reorganize (known as "re-engineering"), you need to configure your marketing department according to a "structural form" (how your area is organized) and a "cultural form" (how your area will act and interact with the rest of the company). The following options should be considered.

Structural Form Options

- Functional form: the marketing manager manages the marketing mix managers.

- Product form: the product manager(s) manages the other marketing mix managers.

- Market form: the market manager(s) manages the marketing mix managers.

- Hybrid form: a combination of functional, product, and/or market forms is used to manage the marketing mix managers.

- Matrix/cross-functional form: the marketing mix managers interact with the marketing manager and other department managers.

- Process form: no department (including marketing) exists as a functional entity; instead, teams are formed in which representatives from departments are shared and work together on a stage/step of a process.

Exhibit 1-2 provides an example of how you might organize a modern marketing department.

Exhibit 1-2

Organization Chart—Cross-Functional Structure
(Industrial Manufacturing)

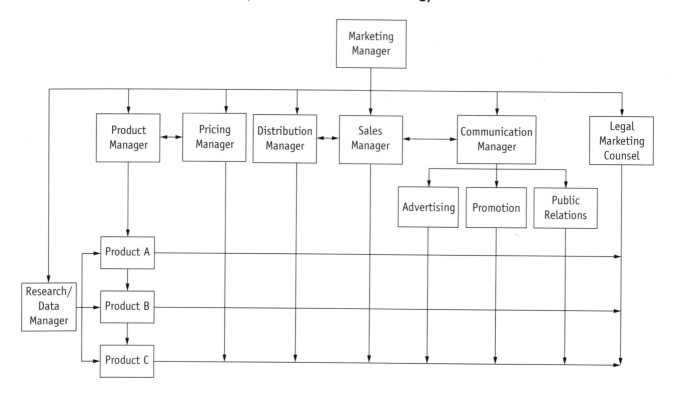

Cultural Form Options

- Centralized or decentralized decision authority

- Micromanagement or macromanagement

- Employee empowerment or management control

The bottom line in building today's marketing department is to get as close to your customers as possible and be able to change quickly to either customer/market, product, or company forces. To accomplish this, it is best to have a marketing structure and culture that places decision-making authority with all levels of staff. This assumes your company is already managing your business according to acceptable business standards and practices. It also assumes you employ marketing individuals with the marketing, business, and management experience to use this authority effectively. It is suggested that your marketing department be as open and cross-functional as possible.

Staff Management

In addition to the structural and cultural change options, changes to staffing may be needed to support your marketing efforts. As a result, the following changes to the marketing department may be required.

Expansion of Staff

- New hires

- Part-time staff

- Freelance help on a per-project basis

- Consultants

Restructuring of Staff

- Shared job responsibilities

- Reassignments

Changes in Job Responsibilities

- New job responsibilities

- Promotions

- Creation of new positions

- Changes in managerial reporting lines

The reporting aspect of your marketing department may need to be discussed if changes are warranted. The information management side of this issue will be profiled in the next section. This section of your plan deals with reporting relationships and/or performance standards that may need to be reviewed. In addition, you should outline training and development actions required to upgrade current staffing resources. You also need to address new and current programs planned for staff training and development of professional or business knowledge.

In preparing and presenting this segment of your marketing plan, you need to convey to the reader what changes will be needed to meet the marketing objectives you have set. It is important to make the case that if you intend to grow and increase your marketing output, your marketing department needs to become more productive and/or have more resources directed at marketing. The cost of these efforts will be discussed in the budget section.

Your organizational plans will be displayed in narrative form in your marketing plan. If productivity performance percentages or sales volume increases (linked to organizational tactics) are needed, as with your organizational goals, you have the freedom to provide whatever data you need to convey the reasoning behind your plans. Re-engineering an organization encompasses more than redesigning your flow chart. If you have questions, consult the *Auditing Markets, Products, and Marketing Plans* book in this series.

Note: Costs associated with staffing and staff structuring will be handled as operational marketing expenses, which are separate from marketing activities, commonly defined as the "cost of marketing."

Marketing Information Systems

In today's marketing world, the timely collection, analysis, and reporting of marketing information is the core of your marketing efforts. The technology used today to manage and access data at both the management and field levels must be an on-line (seamless) process that is quick and easy to use. Therefore, the goal of this section is to demonstrate the level of investment you plan to make in acquiring the desired technological resources. It establishes how marketing information will be used (from a technological standpoint) in supporting your management of your marketing actions.

Elements of Information Systems

This section of your marketing plan focuses on the software, hardware, and data resources that will be acquired and used. The data and the applications for those data (i.e., database marketing) will be profiled in your marketing mix activities under "Research and Data Management Plan."

You need to show the structure in which electronic data will be generated and transmitted. This section of the plan illustrates (usually as a "data mapping flow") the relationships between input and output data points from a customer, marketing, or company user. It also lists the hardware and software applications being selected, as well as the data that will be processed.

Investment

The information system today is a fully automated sales tool that provides marketing (as well as the rest of the company) with information needed to make decisions quickly. These decisions will be made by a human manager or through an intelligent electronic expert system that automatically makes those decisions. This section needs to display the systems you will be using and the policies and procedures that will be needed for data access and distribution.

Areas a marketing information systems (MIS) program should cover are as follows:

- Hardware/software/data sources

- Sales reporting

- Order processing

- Lead management and distribution

- Production, inventory, and shipping reporting

- Customer inquiries, satisfaction, and complaint response measurement

- Marketing cost accounting

- Prospect/customer activity tracking

- Database management and marketing (technical resource)

- Data collection management (point of marketing action)

Your MIS plans will be displayed in narrative form in your marketing plan. If productivity performance percentages or sales volume increases (linked to MIS tactics) are needed, you have the freedom to provide whatever data you need to convey the reasoning behind your plans. If diagrams are needed, a map of the data relationships or the hardware/software configuration selected (in spec sheet form or component listing), you can include those items in your plan, as long as they are not overly detailed. If you wish, you may want to consider attaching them as an exhibit section at the end of your marketing plan document.

Unit 2

Affirming Your Marketing Direction

Your marketing plan is a tactical, one-year marketing instrument. To keep the consistency of marketing planning from year to year and to ensure that long-term goals stay on track, your marketing strategies must be cited. In today's world, traditional strategic thinking and planning is not the overbearing control arm it used to be. In an economic environment where annual rate of return is the end-all measurement of success, a two- to three-year goal may not even be practical. Still, overriding marketing strategies may be warranted to remain loyal to those long-term goals, and therefore the corresponding tactics need to be followed.

The marketing strategies that will drive your marketing plan can be grouped into three areas: overall marketing management, market management, and product management (Exhibit 2-1). Your marketing plan needs to include (in narrative and graphic forms) a section that outlines your marketing intentions from a strategic viewpoint. The three management strategies will act as the underlying forces to direct your upcoming marketing mix activities.

Overall Marketing Management Strategy

The goal of this section is to show the thought process behind how your company will be marketing your products to the marketplace. It is here that you establish the processes and systems you will employ to effectively capture customers, deliver product, and supply the suitable service necessary to satisfy and keep those customers. If you will be investing in a sales automation system, for example, you need to profile the reasoning behind this purchase; the features, benefits, and incentives associated with it; and how it will impact the other marketing mixes.

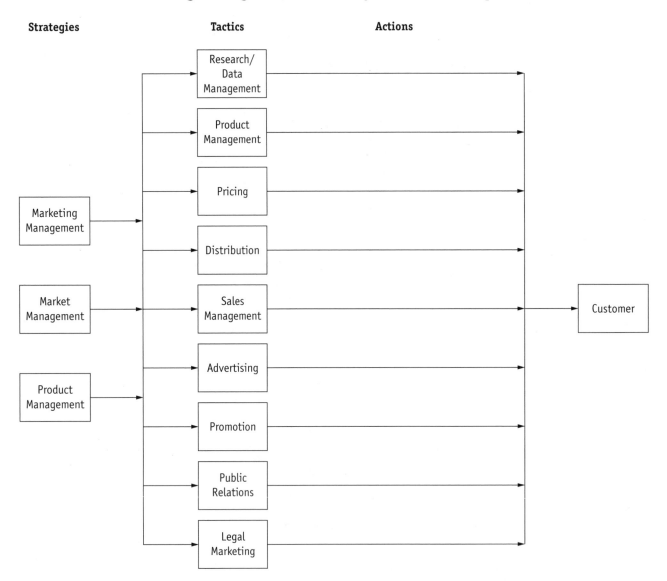

Exhibit 2-1

Marketing Strategies and How They Drive Marketing Tactics

Market Strategy

Your market strategy will consist of defining and identifying your customers and where they are located. The marketplace is made up of several forces. Your strategy must reflect how you will interpret and manage the competition, market dynamics and conditions (i.e., market fluctuations), industry marketing standards, and regulatory and cultural forces. The most important element of any marketplace is the customer. Market segmentation and target marketing strategies need to be covered.

The traditional reliance on market segmenting is being rethought with the desire to focus more on current customers. However, these tools still need to be used, and the blend of new, current, and former customers needs to be determined to establish the methods your marketing plan will employ to prioritize and select your customers.

Your market strategy will go hand in hand with your product strategy, so as you articulate your market strategy, it must agree with your product strategy (Exhibit 2-2).

Exhibit 2-2

Product/Market and Customer Options

(Mix and Select)

Product	Market	Customer
		New Customer-Actual
Current	Current	Current Customer-Actual
		Former Customer-Actual
		New Customer-Type
New	New	Current Customer-Type
		Former Customer-Type

The modern marketing approach is to focus on current customers by managing them like you do your products. The thought is that the cost of maintaining a customer for additional sales opportunities is far less than finding new customers. Current customers can be resold (same product) or sold additional product based on additional needs. These needs come from "relationship marketing," or "customer life cycle marketing." Like product and market life cycles, customers have life cycles too. Depending on the market or industry you serve, the stages a customer goes through can be tracked and targeted by marketing. Thus, your market strategy should take into account not only new customer acquisition, but current customer resecuring. Target marketing tends to focus more on new customers, but it should include all three types of customers.

Target Marketing

The first step is establishing who your market is and where it is located. Although the term *target market* can refer to the identification of a market trade area, the proper use of the term is to refer to smaller and more limited market borders to better manage the area in which you will exist.

Exhibit 2-3 illustrates one method of identifying target markets and customers. Each large circle represents an overall target market, while the smaller circles stand for individual market segments or customers.

Exhibit 2-3

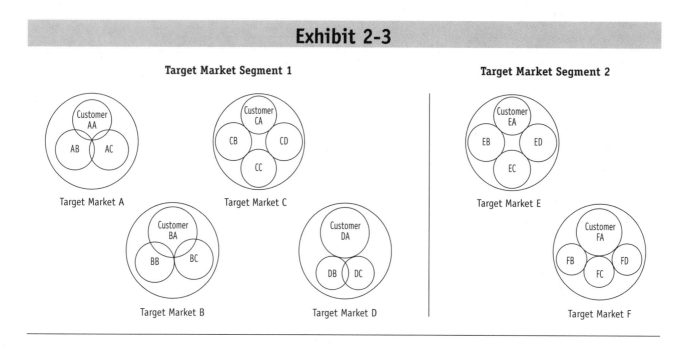

Target Market Segment 1

Target Market Segment 2

Target Market A

Target Market C

Target Market E

Target Market B

Target Market D

Target Market F

Exhibit 2-4 provides you with an exercise in matching products with customer types. The customer profile in the diagram would normally reflect the market segmentation attributes of that customer (age, gender, etc.). Simply indicate which products will appeal to which customers.

Exhibit 2-4

Matching Products to Market and Customer Options
(Mix and Select)

	Target Market					
	New Market			*Current Market*		
	New Customer	Current Customer	Former Customer	New Customer	Current Customer	Former Customer
	Customer Profile	Customer Profile	Customer Profile	Customer Profile	Customer Profile	Customer Profile
Product						
Product						
Total Product Line						

Target Market Selection

The section on market definition (mass vs. segmented) in *Auditing Markets, Products, and Marketing Plans* takes you through the process of identifying and defining your target market. At this point, all you are doing is restating your target definition, establishing your reasons for selecting the target market, and defining the objectives you wish to reach in the target market you have chosen. If you have completed the market analysis, you have this information compiled. You should first record the criteria used for target market selection. Then record the descriptors identifying your target market or markets in Format 6. (Descriptors are demographic or socioeconomic profile variables used to describe and define your target market and customers.)

Format 6

Target Market

Target Market: A			
1: AA		**2:** AB	
Descriptors	**Counts**	**Descriptors**	**Counts**
a. Males	2,648,594	a. Female	9,846,575
b. Age 20–24	4,446,509	b. Age 20–24	3,657,300
c. White	2,367,444	c. Hispanic	5,674,974

Target Market Strategy

Once you have decided who and where, it is time to establish how and why. Developing a target strategy means stating your mission, or niche, within that target market and establishing your company as a "player" in that area (Exhibit 2-5).

Exhibit 2-5

Identifying Target Markets

	Target Market: A			
Customer:	AA	AB	AC	AD
	1	2	3	4
White U.S. males, 20–24, who use hair care products purchased through salons				

Product Strategy

Your product strategy is created by its relationship with the market strategy. Your product strategy will focus on these key points:

- Income sources and products

- Products and the end user

As a company, your goal is to identify and cultivate the various sources for generating income. These sources can be a common product to the end user, a fee to that end user, or a service charge for providing a service enhancement to the end user or another company's end users. The point is, income can be derived from many sources, and marketing can not only cultivate that income but be a source as well (e.g., an automated teller machine can be a distribution channel for a financial services company).

Specifically, a product strategy addresses only the common product line being offered. However, your marketing plan somehow needs to address those alternative income sources that augment common products.

Your product strategy should address your overall product line strategy, as well as individual products. If you're a consumer package product company or service-based company where branding can be employed, that should be part of your strategy. Of course, *branding* is the identity or image your product is intended to project to the customer, as a name and/or visual element, to justify the customer's selection of your product. Your product strategy should reflect market matching, positioning, and penetration plans.

Product/Market Matching

One element of the product strategy is to identify and offer an overview of how your products interact with the markets you serve. This aspect of product strategy development addresses the relationship between product and market. The goal is to be able to clearly define products and customers, so as to isolate which marketing tactics will eventually be deployed.

Exhibit 2-6 is the next step in the exercise begun in Exhibit 2-2. It takes the product/customer mix and links it to your marketing mix. In this exercise, you indicate your strategies by stating your marketing intentions (in text form) in each box. This is considered the strategic overview from which to build out your tactics in the upcoming marketing mix.

Positioning Your Products

To position your products in the marketplace, you need to find out what products are offered by competitors and to consider customers' wants and needs.

Exhibit 2-6

Matching Products/Customers to Marketing Management Options
(Mix and Select)

		Strategies									
		Research/ Data Management	Product Management	Pricing	Distribution	Sales Management	Advertising	Promotion	Public Relations	Legal Marketing	Overall Marketing Management
Product	New Customer	Customer Profile									
	Current Customer	Customer Profile									
	Former Customer	Customer Profile									
Product	New Customer	Customer Profile									
	Current Customer	Customer Profile									
	Former Customer	Customer Profile									
Total Product Line	New Customer	Customer Profile									
	Current Customer	Customer Profile									
	Former Customer	Customer Profile									

You are concerned with showing your products competing in the marketplace, both collectively and individually.

The positioning objectives you select should reflect your target market parameters and the needs and wants of customers in selected target markets. You must then establish your positioning strategy, which you should state in a narrative format such as, "The lite beer that is less filling and tastes great." Possible positioning objectives could be the following:

- Specific product features

- Specific product benefits in terms of problem solving or need satisfaction

- Product price

You can select among many possible positioning strategies. Your products may be positioned in the marketplace against other products. Here are a few examples of possible positioning strategies:

- Differences in features, benefits, or problems solved

- Usage—who uses these products and/or why

- Alternative methods

- Association with a celebrity spokesperson

- Competition pricing

After selecting a positioning strategy, you must attach attributes to the strategy. The choices you have are practically endless; you will need to establish these attributes by using the data found in your market analysis. After you have established your attributes, enter them in Format 7 to display your strategy in a perceptual map form. Also state your strategy in narrative form. (Examples of possible attributes and how they would be entered in Format 7 follow.) In the examples, the attributes chosen are:

A: Inexpensive

B: High Quality

C: Expensive

D: Low Quality

The format provides a method of establishing what your product positioning strategy will be. Your objective is to show how your products rate against the competition by product or product line. Complete the format by defining two characteristics and choosing their opposites as points on the format. For example, in this format the issue of cost is identified with "Expensive" and

Format 7

Product Positioning

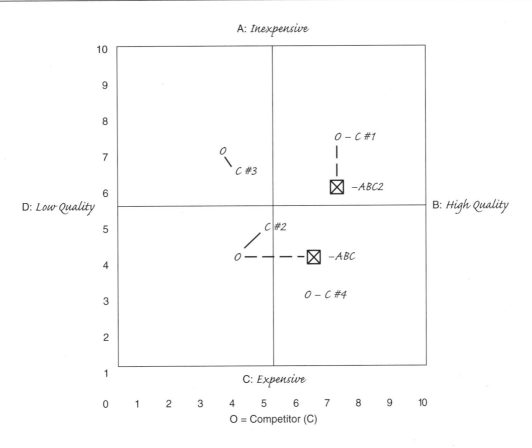

A: *Inexpensive*

D: *Low Quality*

B: *High Quality*

C: *Expensive*

O = Competitor (C)

"Inexpensive" labels. The rating system from 1 to 10 indicates customer perceptions of the products (10 being the best).

Penetration Situation

The next component of your marketing management strategies is your penetration strategy. Your penetration objectives are basically a restatement of your market share goals; however, these objectives are stated as qualitative results of strategy. Your objectives should express what you want to do to enter the market and should reflect both long-term and short-term goals.

How and why you penetrate the market is very important. The method you choose should show how you intend to approach the market and be successful. Your strategy may be one of the following:

- Increase your market share by establishing a growth strategy

- Defend your market share by maintaining what you have

- Control your market share and perhaps your competitors' share by muscling your way into first place

- Maintain your market share by protecting what you have and not worrying about gaining or losing your piece of the pie

Format 8 provides a method of viewing how your penetration strategy will be used for an individual product and the overall product line. Record the actions you will follow for each item under the corresponding time frame.

Format 8

Penetration Strategy

Product	Short Term	Long Term
ABC	Increase market share	Maintain market share
ABC2	Defend market share	Control market share
Overall product line	Increase and defend	Maintain and control

Unit 3

Programming Your Marketing Mix Functions

Units 1 and 2 are devoted to establishing what you want to achieve in the coming year. This unit defines how, when, where, and by whom these goals will be achieved. It is the heart and soul of your marketing plan, the action that delivers on the expectations set. In short, this unit describes the tactical plan (known as the marketing mix) you will implement to reach your marketing goals and objectives.

Each mix component is known as a marketing function. When planning each function, think of how it relates to the overall marketing plan. The nine marketing mix functions are designed as individual plans. Although each function (plan) has specific issues that need to be resolved, they all follow a common format. Each plan sets expectations, budget goals, activities programmed, and monitoring actions used.

Overall Marketing Management Tactical Plan

Your marketing plan, which is driven by the marketing mix plans, must be a totally integrated plan. This means that all marketing mix functions must work together equally as a team, and they must complement each other. Therefore, your opening elements of this tactical plan should offer an overview that outlines how the nine marketing functions will work together to meet your marketing expectations. You need to combine a summary view with an identification of the links or dependencies among the functions.

Strategy, Tactics, and Actions

Your overall marketing management tactical plan is driven by the marketing mix functions. Therefore, the real tactical aspects of a marketing plan are these marketing mix plans. Each plan is considered a process, with actions tied to each process. These actions represent how you are going to market your product to the marketplace.

The individual marketing mix function's plans are driven by the marketing, product, and market strategies profiled in Unit 2. The market strategy particularly will drive your marketing efforts.

Building Your Summary

Similar to the overall marketing plan summary you created in Unit 2, this plan gives a shorter summary, reflecting both the overall summary and each marketing mix plan. In the name of protocol, you need to briefly state your intentions for the nine marketing mix plans.

In today's business climate, your marketing plan summary and the corresponding marketing mix plans should include the following goals:

- Make it simple, yet sophisticated

- Build interactive and integrated marketing actions

- Focus on engaging and partnering with customers

- Cut fat in marketing expenses

- Use new technology

- Become an innovator

- Customize your products and how they are marketed

- Be less creative driven and more response driven

- Demonstrate accountability

Customer Management

The customer aspect of marketing cannot be underrated. Yes, customers are always key, but in today's marketing plans, every marketing mix activity must be linked to customer management.

Customer management is like product management. It is the ability to establish the contributing value of customers by where they are in their life cycle stage and their relationship (current, former, or new) with you. Therefore, your marketing mix plans should focus on the following processes:

- Know what your customers want and offer it

- Use targeted and new direct media actions

- Use nonmedia actions (sports sponsorships, festivals, etc.)

- Augment your communication actions with value-added programs

- Reach customers in the store or where they make the decision to purchase

- Partner with other companies (leverage everyone's expertise)

The bottom line is that your customers need to be treated equally to or as greater value than your products. Each marketing mix function must state the actions planned related to the customer. Your marketing mix plans must differentiate customers, not just products. They must take products to customers, not customers to products. They must reflect the approach of managing your customers, not just your products.

Research and Data Management Plan

In the marketing world, the function of marketing research—and therefore the marketing researcher—has taken on an expanded role. Traditionally, marketing research (as it pertains to the marketing plan) dealt with performing primary or secondary research.

Researchers' role in marketing management was to collect, tabulate, and analyze data and report the findings. The projects typically focused on marketing effectiveness (e.g., advertising), product testing, and customer satisfaction measurement. This is still true, but with the advent of desktop technology, database marketing's expanded role, and the need for on-line data, marketing research is now expected to offer much more.

Technology, Data, and Marketing Research

The data management portion of this function takes available technologies (hardware, software, and acquired data) and determines how they can be used to better identify and predict purchasing patterns and to locate potential customers. The data management side of research tends toward the capture of transaction-based data, which provides insight into a customer's purchasing habits. This is especially true in service and consumer package product industries, but it is less important in the business-to-business and industrial manufacturing industries.

Research/data management provides the following benefits:

- Interfaces between customers and marketing

- Generation of customer data (patterns, trends, etc.) using databases and market segmentation models

- Acquisition of data through traditional research means and data vendors

- Assessment of customer demand and its translation into actions and financial impact

- Interaction with marketing information systems (MIS) and a role as MIS reporting expert

- Measurement of product and marketing effectiveness

This area also acts as the data warehouse king who is looked upon as the keeper of the gate of marketing data. Thus, the marketing research plan must offer traditional research activities alone and in concert with other marketing mix functions, with a strong use of database resources. In addition, database marketing, selling systems, and/or sales automation systems can be tied into this plan to aid or take control of producing data (customer, market, product, and/or marketing-oriented).

Data regarding marketing activity or effectiveness are driven by technology. Because marketing information such as customer profiles and purchasing data can be kept in one place or made readily available, marketing research now takes on a governing position with the other eight marketing functions. Research/data management, with its connections to the company's overall MIS database, can study the buying attributes of customers without having to wait for a report from purchasing, and advertising can get a better picture of who those customers are without having to wait for marketing research to perform research. The marketing research that is conducted still measures customer satisfaction, advertising effectiveness, economic impact, and sales, as well as product testing. Therefore, your marketing research and data management plan blends the traditional requirements of research with the need to control the flow of product, customer, market, and marketing management performance data.

Setting Expectations

The first section of this plan establishes the goals of this function for the year. These goals must coincide with the overall marketing plan goals. In regard to research, it will define what type of routine and ad hoc research projects will be performed and why. In terms of data management, it should focus on building a database and using the data in the most effective manner possible for each marketing function. Format 9 shows one way to present your research objectives and expected results for separate products and the overall product line.

The bottom line is that your research and data management efforts must improve and add value to how your marketing plans are monitored to ensure success.

Many of your goals will be driven by the product life cycle, customer life cycle, and market life cycle models. These models can provide you with a basis for forming goals and tactical plans.

Format 9

Research and Data Management Plan

2000

Product	Objectives	Expected Results
ABC	Learn more about customer satisfaction	Define product capabilities and services to meet customer needs
ABC2	Learn more about how our advertising affects sales	Identify the best way to advertise and sell our products
Overall product line	Perform ongoing research to better understand and monitor forces that affect our marketing	Continue to keep our marketing strategies up-to-date

Establishing Your Budget

After your expectations have been set, you need to establish your budget. Your budget costs are those expenses, outside of salaries, associated with producing research. Cost of data, outside research firm assistance, software (other than the standard package), or any data subscription service should be included. Use Format 10 to establish what you will be spending on each marketing research project. For each product, estimate the cost of the research and the percentage of sales the cost represents.

Format 10

2000

Product	Activity	Cost ($)	Percentage of Sales
ABC	Research project #1, customer satisfaction	10,000	5
ABC2	Research project #2, media response	10,000	5
Total		20,000	10

Marketing Research and Data Management Activities

Once you have set your expectations and your budget, you need to outline your marketing research and data management plans for the year. This will consist of the following elements:

- Market and customer research planned

- Product research planned (current and new products)

- Marketing mix effectiveness planned

- Other marketing-related research planned (e.g., economic impact)

As you build your plan, you need to keep in mind and address how you will deal with marketing mix dependencies and interactions, as well as other department resources. These issues must be resolved, especially in terms of the data management aspect of this plan. The full integration of your marketing efforts can only be accomplished if the links are clearly defined and agreed upon. In addition, the expected results must be defined as they relate to those activities planned. Format 11 shows a way to present this information.

Format 11

2000

Product	Type of Research	Expected Results
ABC	Customer satisfaction measurement	Learn more about customer concerns
ABC2	Advertising/media response tracking	Learn more about advertising effectiveness
Overall product line	Continue to monitor by studying customer needs and media habits	Improve understanding of how well we are marketing our products

Designing Research Projects

What type of research will you be performing in terms of methods and subject matter? In other words, what do you want to monitor and by what means will you do this? Research is used more often in the service and consumer package product industries than in business-to-business industries, because the former are far more complex and unpredictable than other industries. As a result, you must perform some type of research to monitor customer wants and needs.

You will need to determine what tool to use in obtaining research data. These tools, also called techniques, are determined after you know the type of research you want to conduct. You can use any of the following tools: primary research, secondary research, internal database research, or auditing. Use Format 12 to identify the types of research projects you wish to conduct and the techniques you will use, referenced by individual products and the overall product line.

Format 12

2000

Product	Type of Research	Technique
ABC	Customer satisfaction	Primary
ABC2	Advertising/media response	Internal database research
Overall product line	—	Combination of techniques

Planning Data Collection and Processing

The next step is to determine the proper data collection and processing method(s) to use, depending on the information desired and the information available. Complete Format 13 by selecting methods such as qualitative, quantitative, statistical, and nonstatistical (e.g., expert opinion).

Format 13

2000

Product	Type of Research	Data Collection and Processing Method
ABC	Customer satisfaction	Quantitative
ABC2	Advertising/media response	Statistical (rate book research)
Overall product line	—	Combination

Selecting Data Collection Instruments

After you have determined the data collection and processing method(s) you wish to use, you need to select the instruments(s) you will use to collect the data. An instrument is the physical means by which your research data will be obtained. Complete Format 14 by selecting instruments such as mall intercepts, focus groups, and mail or telephone surveys.

Choosing Types of Tabulation and Analysis

The objective of this exercise is to establish what types of tabulation and analysis activities you will use to manipulate the data collected. Format 15 provides a method of selecting the proper tabulation and analysis programs to use for the coming year. Choose one of the following: cross tabulation/summary tabulation, statistical modeling analysis, or other.

Format 14

2000

Product	Type of Research	Data Collection Instrument
ABC	Customer satisfaction	Telephone survey and follow-up
ABC2	Advertising/media response	Other
Overall product line	—	Combination

Format 15

2000

Product	Type of Research	Data Tabulation and Analysis Tools
ABC	Customer satisfaction	Cross tabulation
ABC2	Advertising/media response	statistical modeling analysis
Overall product line	—	Combination

Evaluating the Effectiveness of Research and Data Management Actions

Each marketing function will have a measurement activity planned. This is to constantly monitor the effectiveness of the research and data management planned are meeting the goals set. If not, changes can be made quickly, if results dictate additional or different research or data management actions. In Unit 6, an area is devoted to helping you plug research data back into the marketing plan.

Product Management and Development Plan

The core of any company is the products or services it provides to the marketplace. Proper product management is a critical part of any marketing effort. Your product line plan must mix and balance current product successes with enhancements to those products and/or entirely new product additions, as well as with the deletion of old products. Products, which typically account for the majority of income sources and the level of income generated, must be reviewed constantly to ensure that they are reaching their utmost potential and meeting customer needs.

Expectations and Budgeting

In developing your product plan, you first need to set your product expectations and establish your budget. Your expectations normally will center around current and new product features and benefits—making sure they meet the needs of customers and making sure customers can recognize those features and benefits. Your costs usually focus on any research or development (e.g., engineering) expenses associated with changes to your products. Depending on how you allocate and assign costs (manufacturing, technical development, etc.), your marketing dollars will need to be adjusted to reflect long-term amortization of the research and development costs or as a one-time allocation amount. Testing expenses commonly fall under your marketing research budget. If your product plans are to concentrate on your existing products, your costs will be minimal.

Many of your goals will be driven by the product life cycle, customer life cycle, and market life cycle models, which can provide a basis on which to form tactical plans. Use Formats 16 and 17 to set forth your development budget and objectives, respectively.

Format 16

Product Development Plan

			2000
Product	Activity	Cost (Gross)	Percentage of Sales
ABC	Maintaining product line	$10,000	1.5
ABC2	Enhancing product line	$5,000	.5
Total		$15,000	2.0

Your product plans may include any changes in procedures or policy that govern how your product is marketed (internal use) or how your product is used

Format 17		
		2000
Product	**Objectives**	**Expected Results**
ABC	Update	Increase value, extend life cycle, continue solid sales
ABC2	Enhance	Fine-tuning only
Overall product line	Refine product appeal	Improve the attractiveness and benefits of product offerings

by the customer (external use). Legal issues will be covered later in this book, but if your product plans include changes that need to be communicated in terms of usage, documentation changes should be included in your plans. For products from the consumer package product industry, where branding plays a major role, costs associated with branding fall under advertising, promotions, and/or public relations.

Current Product Line Plans

Your first responsibility is to your present product offerings. These products are currently in the marketplace and must be supported and sold. Your objective is to assess what changes, if any, need to be made to make sure your products continue to sell and generate adequate revenues. In your product audit and product strategy, you already determined your products' life cycle stages and prescribed corresponding marketing tactics for them.

In addressing the state of your current product line and establishing your product tactics for the year, you need to look at what changes are warranted. If changes are necessary, options for product line modification may include the following:

- Altering or refining the features and benefits (reemphasizing issues)

- Reformulating or retooling the technical origin of the product substance (new, improved, or updated version)

- Adding value (packaging with other products or related services)

- Adjusting to pricing and/or costing (lower or higher)

- Repositioning in product line or against the competition

- Deleting or phasing out product(s) from line

- Adding new or replacement products (note new product development)

Format 18 provides a method of demonstrating your product management plan for current products.

Format 18		
Product	Objectives	Expected Results
ABC	No change	Maintain market share
ABC2	Product alteration	Increase sales
Overall product line	Slight modifications	Continue growth

Product Branding Plan

As mentioned earlier, if branding is part of your product plans, separate attention needs to be placed on that aspect of your product marketing. Your branding plan will focus on the same issues as those stated for your products. When branding is a consideration, your focus becomes the product brand (or identity). The product itself becomes more of a technical by-product and has little or no impact on your marketing efforts. However, if your product changes, its brand must be adjusted to reflect that change. The key thing to remember in planning your brand program is that brand developments must match your product plans through brand reinforcement, brand repositioning, and brand modification. Your branding options can include the following:

- Maintaining position

- Repositioning or inventing the brand

- Multibranding (private label versus brand name)

- Positioning a brand extension

- Modifying or replacing the brand

Branding can be applied to all industries, especially consumer package product and service sectors. Format 19 shows a method of presenting your branding plan.

Format 19		
Product	**Plan**	**Expected Results**
ABC	Brand reinforcement	Continued strong awareness
ABC2	Modification	Slight enhancement to keep us up-to-date with trends
Overall product line	Small changes to branding strategy	Strengthen overall market share

Planning Product Packaging

Packaging, like branding, is an extension of your product developments and must reflect those developments. The purpose of packaging is to protect as well as draw attention to your product offerings. Packaging becomes more important in the consumer package product environment because the end user is selecting and purchasing the item. Your goal is to make sure your product plan, branding plan, and packaging plan are fully integrated. When making your packaging plan, you need to consider the following:

- What message the package communicates

- Usefulness of the package

- Cost of the packaging and shipping

- Appearance of the package at the point of sale

The key consideration in all of your product planning is to identify the other marketing mix dependencies. Your marketing plan needs to be integrated. To accomplish this, each marketing mix plan must address not only its specific risks and rewards, but how it impacts the other functions. This includes defining the resources or capabilities needed from those functions. In addition, other departments such as technical research and development must be included in your plans.

New Product Development

If your current product plans include a new product entry as either a replacement for a phased-out product or an entirely new product category, product development needs to have special attention. To develop a new product, you need to manage not only the marketing aspects of product marketing, but production, research and development (engineering), and cost accounting. You can, of course, use external product acquisition as an option if internal means are not as attractive.

The process of creating a product development plan begins with a product development process. A product development process is provided in *Auditing Markets, Products, and Marketing Plans*. That process includes the following stages (shown in a brief overview):

- Idea formulation, concept assessment, and acceptance

- Product development commencement

- Designing and planning

- Product building

- Procedural development

- Testing and modification

- Implementation

Planning New Product Introductions

You need to determine how you will handle new product line additions. (New product releases require special attention when implementation is planned during the current year.)

Your plans should describe the impact and contributions of all the marketing mix functions. This will include how, when, where, and through whom you will be introducing and releasing your new products. Any changes to your product branding and packaging plans need to be resolved. This includes defining other marketing mix and department involvement in bringing the new products to life. Use Format 20 to set forth your new product plans.

Format 20

Product	Plan	Expected Results
ABC22	*Develop using internal R&D resources*	*Continue to augment product choices for customers*
—	—	—
Overall product line	*New product introduction*	*Maintain product line growth rates*

Your new product plan should focus on product/project plans already under way (for entry in the current year) and development activities for the coming year's release. It should measure impact on total sales and individual products.

Most new products almost always take away from an existing product or products in your product line and, as a result, your impact analysis needs to adjust for all product sales.

Planning Service Support (Products Only)

When you are selling a physical product in the consumer package product industry, service generally means after-sale support or a value-added feature. Its purpose is to enhance the value of obtaining your product and to provide you (when appropriate) with another possible revenue source. (If the latter is true, you need to add this other income source to your sales and revenue projections.) In any case, service enhancement is a way of making your product better. Service enhancements may include a telephone support line, repair and maintenance, or training in product use.

Product and Market/Customer Matching

For the purposes of your marketing plan, you should present your product plans referenced to the customers you are targeting. This brings closure to your product plans by stating who will buy your product in increased frequency, volume, and price points (demand analysis). Product, branding, packaging, and service support should all be included in matching offerings with customers.

Exhibit 3-1

Product Performance By Target Market

	New Market			Current Market		
	New Customer	Current Customer	Former Customer	New Customer	Current Customer	Former Customer
	Customer Profile	Customer Profile	Customer Profile	Customer Profile	Customer Profile	Customer Profile
Product						
Product						
Total Product Line						

To demonstrate this matching, use Exhibit 3-1 to cross-reference your product plans to your customer types and status. At each point of intersection, enter the reasoning for the connection. In addition, you need to show how the other marketing mix functions interface with your products. Exhibit 3-2 displays, at a glance, your marketing tactics as they relate to each existing and new product being offered.

Exhibit 3-2

Tactical Product-Position Matching

		Tactics									
		Research/ Data Management	Product Management	Pricing	Distribution	Sales Management	Advertising	Promotion	Public Relations	Legal Marketing	Overall Marketing Management
Product	New Customer Customer Profile										
	Current Customer Customer Profile										
	Former Customer Customer Profile										
Product	New Customer Customer Profile										
	Current Customer Customer Profile										
	Former Customer Customer Profile										
Total Product Line	New Customer Customer Profile										
	Current Customer Customer Profile										
	Former Customer Customer Profile										

The product life cycle concept (introduction, growth, maturity, and decline) will drive your product marketing plans. The four stages of a product's life are linked to sales, costs, profits, customer behavior, and competitor characteristics, then to marketing objectives and individual marketing mix plans (product, price, distribution, and advertising/customer sales promotions). This is a very basic concept, but the principles can form and lead you to appropriate marketing planning tactics. For companies in the business-to-business or industrial manufacturing world, product life cycle marketing may have less impact. Still, the concept can be applied to those industries, depending on your customers (dealers, distributors, or resellers) and their use of your products.

Monitoring Product Management Activity

To ensure your product plans are carried out as designed and/or track the effectiveness of your tactics, you need to monitor your product actions. You need to measure how well your product plans are performing. Assuming your plans are on target, this effort ensures you stay on track. If your plans fall short or exceed expectations, your monitoring and reporting can offer timely ideas for change and quick responses to unforeseen issues.

Service as a Product

For those businesses that operate in the service industry, product marketing can still be applied. When you are marketing a service, you are dealing with an intangible. To stimulate the customer's desire to purchase your service, you must treat it like a tangible product. You need to think in terms of features and the corresponding benefits (even branding), as well as product incentives.

Although quality is an aspect of all products and services, services are especially sensitive to customer satisfaction. How you deliver the service to your customer is critical. Therefore, your product plans need to focus heavily on service quality and service response.

It is up to you whether you call this section of your marketing plan a product plan or a service plan. The key thing to remember is to take the product issues that have been discussed in this section and apply them to your services. A service is an income source and needs to be treated with great care. Your customer must hold your service at a high level of importance. To make this happen, you need to push your service as though it were a tangible product.

Pricing Plan

Hundreds of books have been written on how to form pricing policies; determining the price for a product or service can be complex. However, pricing is based on two things: product costs and the price the market will bear, i.e., pricing attractive enough for customers to purchase the product. Depending on whether you are in the consumer package product, business-to-business/industrial manufacturing, or service industries, your pricing options will differ.

The actual costs are usually easy to determine, but linking those costs to volume of product sold and amortizing those plant costs can be very subjective. The same is true in trying to determine what the customer will pay to obtain the product or service you are offering. Once you have determined unit cost and price, you are ready to place "value" on your product line offerings. It is this value/price that drives your sales and revenue forecasts and profitability projections.

Although pricing is usually integrated into your product management and has very little cost associated with it, pricing needs to be defined separately because of its importance to every other marketing move.

Expectations and Budgeting

Because pricing is essentially a part of product management, it has no budget. However, because pricing is such an important element of a business's success, separate objectives must be established. Format 21 provides a method of establishing your pricing budget for the coming year. Pricing alone does not often incur cost, but a format is offered here because pricing falls under the heading of product management and we are trying to keep our marketing functions consistent. Record your pricing activities or tactics in Format 21, and remember to include any costs associated with them.

Format 21

Pricing Plan

			2000
Product	Activity	Cost	Percentage of Sales
ABC	No change	—	0
ABC2	Modify	—	0
Total		—	0

Once your budget is set, your next step is to establish your objectives for the coming year. Although pricing seems simple on paper, the issue of establishing a price for a product or overall product line can be risky. Many of your goals will be driven by the product life cycle, customer life cycle, and market life cycle models, which can provide you with a basis for tactical plans. Use Format 22 to record your pricing objectives.

Format 22

Product	Objectives	Expected Results
ABC	Keep the same price	Maintain solid sales
ABC2	Drop price	Enhance pricing value and improve sales to promote growth
Overall product line	Make pricing a small part of the marketing mix	Keep sales steady and profits high

Determining the Pricing Formula

Once your product line plan is established, you need to attach a value to those products. You do this by establishing your gross and net costs to produce the product. Then you determine the price level that will cover your costs, provide suitable profits, and attract customers. Format 23 provides a method of demonstrating your pricing programs.

Format 23

Product	Pricing Formula	Expected Results
ABC	No change	steady sales
ABC2	Drop pricing, keep cost at same level	Improved sales
Overall product line	Change pricing to meet the needs of customers but still cover costs	Continued sales volume growth

Setting Your Pricing Tactics

Once your pricing formulation has been determined, your price plan needs to be set. This plan deals with converting the pricing formula into product pricing policies for the year.

The following tactics could be deployed to take your products to your customers:

- Price alteration (lower or higher)

- Price discounting

- Cost cutting

- Special pricing (limited time offers or product phase-outs)

- Price repositioning

- Target pricing programs (rebates or promotional tie-ins)

Your pricing plan must reflect your product plan. It is important to keep in mind how the price compares to what the product is offering. Price can even be a product feature, as it is for luxury automobiles. In this case, a car is priced high to reflect its position, although in reality the basic costs to produce a mid-priced car are not much less. For each product, you need to establish the base price and discount policy (quantity breaks or allowances for returns).

Format 24 provides a method to demonstrate your pricing programs. As with your product plans, the product life cycle stages at which your products currently exist or will exist will help you establish your pricing tactics.

Format 24

Product	Plan	Expected Results
ABC	Maintain current price	Maintain sales trends
ABC2	Adjust price positioning to competition's	Be more competitive and increase sales
Overall product line	Set pricing to fit each product's situation	Offer special pricing to generate sales throughout the year

Establishing Price/Cost Structure

The final part of your pricing plan will be the resulting pricing structure by product. The objective is to establish the profitability of your products, based on the price plan you have selected. Format 25 provides a method of demonstrating the profitability of your pricing programs.

The consumer package product, business-to-business/industrial manufacturing, and service industries all have special circumstances that will alter pricing structure. In fact, certain sectors of each industry present special issues. However, the basic structures of all inflows—sales minus allowances and the cost of materials (gross costs, cost of goods sold, etc.) equals profit, and therefore the margin—follow the same business flow. The key dynamic is the inflow caused by price to the customer. Regardless of your business, the role of pricing and the pricing plan are the core drivers to a profitable and sales-generating marketing plan.

Format 25		
	Product: *ABC*	Product: *ABC2*
Volume (units)	*1+*	*1+*
Price ($)	*10.00*	*8.00*
Discount* ($)	*No volume discounting*	*Same*
Revenue ($)	*10.00*	*8.00*
Gross Costs ($)	*2.00*	*2.00*
Gross Profit ($)	*8.00*	*6.00*
Gross Margin (%)	*80*	*75*
*Discounting is based on many factors, such as volume, package features, etc.		

Pricing Dependencies

To successfully establish a pricing plan, you need to clearly define your relationship with other marketing mix managers and department managers. Specifically, the product manager and his or her tactical plans need to work as one with you and your plans. Research is another function that needs careful consideration. If price testing or research is warranted, your pricing plans need to reflect those actions. The biggest dependency comes from the connections with finance and accounting. These areas need to work with you to determine costing, risk, and allowance issues. They will also assist you in establishing the proper pricing threshold (along with customer research).

Other departments that may need to be involved with pricing would be production, legal marketing, and even finance. Individuals from all of these departments act as resources to consult in ensuring that pricing is fair, profitable, competitive, and attractive to the customer.

Pricing Management

In planning your pricing actions, you need to include any pricing policies and tracking systems needed to guard against loss of focus. Setting a pricing structure and following that structure will only work if the proper guidelines are used and enforced. It is so easy to determine price points and then make exceptions. Although there are times when pricing adjustments need to be available, they should be built into the structure beforehand. The point is that pricing policies may need to be created, published, and adopted to ensure that the revenues planned materialize as planned.

To properly monitor your pricing actions, you need to again track both the pricing structure performance and the policies driving the use of that structure. Use both quantitative and qualitative instruments to determine whether your pricing plans are working as they were designed to and, if not, whether it is because of the design or because the design is not being followed.

Distribution Plan

The function of distribution used to be easy to define. Today, with the various delivery systems and multiple logistical channel options, distribution is no longer a quick plan. On-line inventory tracking, automated fulfillment, and faster transportation are all changing the face of distribution. Your distribution options will differ depending on whether you are in the consumer package product, business-to-business/industrial manufacturing, or service industries.

The role of distribution for the different industries also varies. In the consumer package product industry, distribution's role is complex because of the changes in retailing. No longer do specialty stores or local store chains rule the landscape. Today, category killers like Lowe's or Office Depot direct the business approach in the world of marketing. Essentially, a distribution plan in this industry consists of the following options:

- Producer direct to the customer

- Producer to the retailer and then to the customer

- Producer to a wholesaler, the retailer, and then to the customer

- Producer to an agent (e.g., manufacturer's representative), to the wholesaler, to the retailer, and finally to the customer

In the business-to-business/industrial manufacturing industry, your company's role can be that of either a producer or the distribution source itself. Your primary options are as follows:

- Producer to the industrial user

- Producer to the distributor or dealer, then to the industrial user

- Producer to an agent, and then to the industrial user

Within the service industry, distribution may or may not exist. Historically, distribution plans were omitted as part of the marketing plan in this area, because a service is intangible and distribution was nonexistent. However, distribution can be interpreted as any manner in which a service is delivered to a customer. The transmission of data (electronic data transfer) or signals to produce an action for a price can be considered a version of distribution. As a result, distribution can be included as part of a service-based marketing plan.

Setting Expectations and Budgets

Like all the marketing mix plans, the distribution plan needs objectives and budget parameters. Depending on how your company defines distribution, your budget may include warehousing, shipping, and transportation or just one or two of these areas. Again, the life cycle stages of your products will assist you in defining your product-specific distribution plans.

Format 26 provides a method for establishing what you will spend on product distribution in the coming year. Complete the format by listing the activity/tactic you expect to use with the estimated cost of that action and the percentage of sales that cost represents.

Format 26

Distribution Plan

2000

Product	Activity	Cost ($)	Percentage of Sales
ABC	Same plan	10,000	1.0
ABC2	Same plan	10,000	1.0
Total		20,000	2.0

Once your budget is established, your next step is to determine your distribution objectives. These should include such items as coverage, outlet types, timing, and direct or indirect delivery. Format 27 provides a method of defining your objectives by product or overall product line.

	Format 27	
		20*00*
Product	**Objectives**	**Expected Results**
ABC	*Continue current activities*	*Maintain flow of product with no disruptions*
ABC2	*Same*	*Same*
Overall product line	*Use combined system*	*Achieve stable sales*

Selecting Delivery Channels

To this point you have dealt with determining what you are going to offer the customer. Now you must decide how you will get your products into the hands of that customer or user in the most cost-effective and efficient way. Selecting channels is essentially the tactical element of your distribution plan. Therefore, the following three steps and the options available within those steps represent the tactical side of your distribution plan.

First, decide on the *delivery system*. The options provided earlier outline the channels available. A delivery system should include the relationship with sales and other departments (e.g., inventory). For example, if a sales automation system is being employed, distribution will play a major role in that system.

Second, determine the *method of delivery*. This aspect of your distribution plan addresses the actual, or physical, manner in which the product or service will be delivered. The following options are available for inventory fulfillment and shipping:

- Semiautomated delivery systems

- Fully automated or on-line delivery systems

The following options are available for transportation or transmission:

- Highway, railroad, water, or air carrier

- Underground/over-ground flow

- Electronic transfer

Third, identify the *destination* to which you will be shipping your product for purchase. This can be done through indirect or direct means.

Destination (indirect)

- Distributors

- Dealers and resellers

- Other manufacturers

- Franchises

- Brokers/agents

- Telemarketing and fulfillment operators

Destination (direct)

- Person-to-person (door-to-door)

- Mail order (catalogs, TV home shopping)

- Automatic vending

- Internet, on-line services, and interactive/point-of-purchase kiosks

- Retail outlets (department stores, specialty stores, etc.)

- Wholesale outlets (category killers, factory outlets, wholesale showrooms, etc.)

Other options may include joint ventures. In this situation, you can co-op or share in the distribution and marketing efforts with another company. This method is often used in private label arrangements where identical products are marketed under different names.

Format 28 provides a method of demonstrating your distribution plan's delivery channels. You can verify your channel selection by matching each with the product's ultimate point of purchase. Then link the purchase point with the ultimate customer. Format 29, which is not shown in your completed marketing plan, can help you do this.

Format 28

Product	Delivery Channel	Expected Results
ABC	Sell/ship directly to stores	Continued steady sales
ABC2	Same, but offer specials through direct mail	Same
Overall product line	Combination of channels	Continued strong sales growth

Format 29			
Product	**Delivery Channel**	**Origin of Purchase**	**Market**
ABC	Sell/ship direct	Local retail store	Retail shopper
ABC2	Same	Same	Same
Overall product line	Sell/ship direct	In-store	Retail shopper

Managing Your Distribution Plan

The distribution plan describes the entire distribution operation. The main goal is to make sure that the channel you've selected is beneficial for all parties. In the consumer package product industry, for example, you will often have a multilevel distribution network. You ship your product to a retail chain's distribution center, which in turn ships your product to the chain's stores. Your distribution plan should include the overall configuration of the delivery system as well as procedures for inventory control, shipping and handling, and billing. Format 30 provides a method of establishing how you will manage your distribution activities.

Format 30		
Product	**Distribution Plan**	**Expected Results**
ABC	Employ an automated system that handles everything using internal staff resources	Faster, easier, less expensive distribution
ABC2	Same	Same
Overall product line	Use a computerized, integrated system Control the entire system from one point	Improved efficiency in delivering goods

Distribution needs to be integrated with your other marketing mix functions. Advertising, for example, can play a major role in packaging and direct response. Other departments, such as warehouse facility and inventory systems management, need to be involved with all aspects of your distribution plans.

You need to determine the status of your vendors' contracts. Evaluate how well the relationships between you and your distribution vendors have worked. Check expiration dates of contracts and financial ramifications of the relationships if there is any doubt.

Like all your marketing mix functions, you need to employ a tracking system to ensure that your distribution activities are meeting your marketing demands. This information will allow you to alter your plans if problems materialize.

Sales Management and Selling Plan

The purpose of marketing, as it relates to planning, is to get your product to your customer as easily and cost-effectively as possible. Selling is the action that holds your marketing plan together. Although the act of selling plays a key role in the success of your marketing plans, marketing activities should not be aimed solely toward sales and salespeople. Sales should be balanced with the other eight marketing functions to form a well-supported and integrated marketing plan. Your sales and selling options will differ depending on your industry (consumer package product, business-to-business/industrial manufacturing, or service).

In today's high-tech marketing environment, sales management—and therefore your sales plan—is experiencing great change. The advent of the Internet, on-line sales automation and delivery systems, and laptop technology are changing how sales are made, but the goals and principles are the same.

The process of sales management starts with deciding who will sell your products (sales force development). Motivating your sales force by means of sales incentives and compensation for their performance based on quota levels is next. Then you must establish how they will sell, to what customers they will sell, and what their sales territory in terms of physical area and/or key accounts will be. Finally, you need to establish how you will manage these salespeople, the sales they generate, and their overall sales performance.

Sales Expectations and Budgeting

First you need to set your objectives. Of course, your sales activities will be driven by your sales and profit forecasts. But your objectives should include more than just meeting quotas. Your sales and selling plans should include staff development in terms of product, market, and selling knowledge. They should focus on the interaction between all marketing mix functions.

Many of your goals will be driven by the product life cycle, customer life cycle, and market life cycle models, which can provide you with a basis for forming tactical plans. Use Format 31 to record your planned activities.

Format 31		
Sales Management Plan		
		20*00*
Product	**Objectives**	**Expected Results**
ABC	*Improve salespersons' ability to sell more products*	*Obtain sales forecasts*
ABC2	*Same*	*Same*
Overall product line	*Make sales staff more aware of product benefits*	*Generate predicted sales volume and revenue levels*

Your defined budget must reflect your commitment to meeting your expectations. It should include everything except compensation (base or bonus), which is covered in either your marketing operational budget or your company's overall overhead expenses. Format 32 provides a method of establishing what you will be spending on the management of your sales over the coming year. Complete the format by filling in the activities you expect to use with the estimated cost of those actions and the percentage of sales the costs represent.

Format 32			
			2000
Product	**Activity**	**Cost ($)**	**Percentage of Sales**
ABC	Product tracking	5,000	2.5
ABC2	Product tracking	5,000	4.5
Total		10,000	7.0

Sales Systems Selection

In the past, the definition of sales systems was the process by which a salesperson coordinated prospecting, presenting, closing, and delivering the desired goods. Today, sales systems comprise an integrated on-line computer system that enables a salesperson to market a product at the push of a button (almost!). Salespeople no longer prospect; they field inquiries and service and support customers.

A salesperson today can make a sales call with a complete record of the customer's sales history, up-to-date information about the market and competitors, detailed product specifications, current (by-the-minute) price sheets and inventory reports, and all other data needed to close the sale. This is all done using a state-of-the-art sales automation system. It is possible because of the availability of new and more powerful portable computers that store huge amounts of information and sport high-speed modems, cellular hookups, wireless transmission, and cutting-edge software. With a direct on-line link to the home office, a salesperson can place real-time orders.

Sales automated systems can integrate research and data management, advertising (using direct marketing/response), distribution, and customer service to identify the customer and the customer's behavior. The end result is that you can configure a selling system that balances modern technology with the human interaction of customer demand in a package that meets your sales goals.

Another form of sales system is a totally electronic system known as an "expert system." Such systems rely on preprogrammed logic that makes automatic decisions about the customer's likelihood of becoming a closed sale. It has artificial intelligence to define and select customers who will buy your products.

Using your marketing information systems resources, you need to build (with the help of a vendor) a fully integrated automated sales system that focuses on the following key elements:

- Database management (list selection/data acquisition and merging, customer identification, and purchasing predictions)

- Sales/lead generation (inquiry production, distribution, and reporting)

- Order processing (order entry, accounts receivable, shipping, inventory change reporting, and fulfillment/follow-up communications)

- Customer support and services (satisfaction, call management, and problem reporting)

Organizing Your Sales Structure

Once you have determined the system under which you will operate your sales and selling activities, you need to determine the structure in which that system will operate. The structure establishes the focus of your sales efforts. It is important to define how you will approach sales and selling. The following are options you may wish to use:

- Product sales approach

- Market sales approach

- Customer-specific approach

- Sales transaction approach

- Combination approach

The trick to selecting an approach is finding one that allows you to respond quickly to market, product, and customer issues. Obviously, the customer approach or an approach that features customer management is a key marketing driver. You need to select the approach that will be the most productive and efficient way to generate sales given the industry and the situation in which you operate. Your structure relates back to the system you have selected.

Marketing and Sales Management

Although we have said that structure concentrates on how you will arrange your sales department, it also means how your sales department will be managed.

There can be no more divisive or critical issue in marketing management than sales management.

The issue is whether the marketing manager should manage the sales manager, whether they should be equal, or whether sales should manage marketing. Although each of these management structures has been successful, the structure that provides the most consistent, controlled/low-risk balance is that in which the marketing manager manages the sales manager. Marketers have argued about this relationship for years. When sales managers control how the other marketing mix functions operate, you get a slanted view of marketing. If sales runs marketing, you typically get low-priced products that may not be profitable but are easy to sell. By having marketing run sales, you get a balanced attack. The bottom line is the act of selling, which is number one in marketing, should not be confused with the act of managing sales.

Sales Staff Management and Development

Once you have selected the system and structure for your sales and selling plans, you need to define the role of your sales staff. Although some businesses may do away totally with sales and focus on technology and/or customer service, it can be assumed that most will employ some form of sales staff. Assuming a sales force is needed to move your products, you need to determine how you will manage the staff, along with the technology of generating sales.

Depending on the life cycle stage your products are in and the industry in which you compete, the role of your sales force will differ. For example, your sales force may have to contend with selling directly to stores and seeking to obtain shelf or floor space, which can entail slotting fees. In this situation, its role may include negotiating and order taking. Salespeople may be required to carry some type of portable laptop to record product sales using bar coding or data entry. In any case, your sales staff will be required to perform high- and low-level activities. They must be trained on the equipment to perform to the standards required.

Your plans must focus on selecting the best people who represent the best sales methods available. In planning your sales force development, consider the use of internal versus independent representatives, sales staff size, and recruitment and training of sales staff. Training is usually a major cost consideration. Expenses include training activities, travel, and lodging.

Format 33 provides a method of determining how you will configure your sales force. Select the development activity that best fits your needs.

Format 33

Product	Plan	Expected Results
ABC	Use internal staff of 300 Expand sales staff by 50	Meet target sales forecasts and improve salespeople's image
ABC2	Same, but with no expansion in sales force	Same
Overall product line	Modest growth in sales staff	Attain sales goals and make sales staff more professional

Planning Internal Sales Promotions

Sales promotions, a subcomponent of promotion, can be separated into two types: external sales promotions, directed at customers as an incentive to buy more, and internal sales promotions, directed at the salesperson as an incentive to sell more. External sales promotion as a marketing mix function will be covered later. In internal sales promotions, you must design an attractive package to motivate your salespeople. While external sales promotions usually consist of value-added incentives, internal sales promotions generally offer cash bonuses or material incentives such as trips. In the consumer package product industry, your sales capacity is dictated by the stores you service; they tell you what, where, and when they will sell your products. Therefore, your sales promotions will often be directed at store chains as well as your sales force.

There are two basic types of internal sales promotions: bonuses and special incentives. Bonuses are linked to a salesperson's present compensation package, and special incentives are tied in to a specific, time-based sales quota. Special incentives are used when trying to move a product quickly. The salesperson's additional compensation can come in the form of cash awards, prizes, and sales premiums.

Use Format 34 to demonstrate what types of internal sales promotions you will employ.

Format 34

Product	Plan	Expected Results
ABC	straight bonus	Meet sales goals
ABC2	Same	Same
Overall product line	Keep compensation balanced with sales volume	Generate revenues and keep sales staff happy

Planning Salesperson Compensation

Most good salespeople are motivated by income. As a result, you need to design a compensation program that fits your financial resources and produces positive return for a salesperson's efforts. Historically, the consumer package product industry has used low-pressure salespeople because companies in this market depend primarily on stores to sell products, and the salespeople are not directly responsible for the end sale to the customer. In developing a compensation plan, you need to realize the limitations of your salespeople in selling your product. Your compensation package must reward a salesperson for service to the store as well as for unit sales. Use Format 35 to record your compensation plans.

Format 35		
Product	**Plan**	**Expected Results**
ABC	Straight salary	Steady sales without pressure on customers
ABC2	Same	Same
Overall product line	Salaried sales force with limited volume incentives	Steady sales without pressure on customers

Assigning Sales Territories

How you establish where your sales force will sell is important. You must assign salespeople to territories that are fair to both you and them. In the consumer package product industry you should design your territories using a formula that focuses on time management, customer service, sales, and costs.

Although territories are commonly used, key accounts, especially high-volume customers, need to be included in the equation. In fact, the best method is often to base sales territories on major accounts. Market-based assignments are also beneficial. In this situation, a salesperson represents customer types based on purchasing habits, competition, or any other market-driven dynamic. The key issue is to select one or a combination of the three assignment methods to define the most productive selling formula.

Format 36 provides a method of determining how you define your sales territories. Link each product to a salesperson and then establish how that person will service the sales territories. This may be done by geographic area, based on physical area and customer density, or by key customer accounts.

Format 36

Product	Salesperson A: *J. Doe*	Salesperson B: *J. Smith*	Expected Results
ABC	Sell by geographic area only	Same	Strong coverage across country
ABC2	Sell by key customer accounts only	Sell by geography only	Same, with customers served in the Chicago area
Overall product line	Use both methods of defining territories	Same	Happy customers and solid sales

Sales Tactics

The tactical aspect of your sales plan may include the components we have discussed so far. In addition, however, other issues necessitate the use of the following approaches:

- Sales methods (selling process)
- Sales techniques (presentation process)
- Sales comparisons (competition)
- Combination

Format 37

Sales Tactics

Product	Tactic	Expected Results
ABC	Using our new sales Automatron process, market in person to customers	Lower cost per call by 2% Lower cost per call by 1%
ABC2	Same	Same
Overall product line	Same	Same

Tracking Sales Activity

A sales manager needs to monitor the sales activities of his or her salespeople, as well as to monitor and predict sales. Salespeople are typically tracked by the sales process they go through to produce a sale and by the number of calls, contacts, and orders they must generate to reach their sales quotas.

Because of the nature of the various industries, tracking sales activity is of different importance to sales managers in each market. However, any sales manager who is responsible for overseeing and/or reporting on sales activity should monitor each salesperson.

There are several methods to track sales activity. The first examines the sales cycle (approach, fact finding, demonstration/proposal, and close). Another way to track activity is to examine sales techniques. Are your salespeople selling packaged product lines or individual products? You can recognize sales actions taken within a specified time period. These may include number of phone calls, number of sales calls, or average dollar size per sale.

Format 38 shows a method of tracking sales activity per salesperson by dollar amount.

Format 38

2000

Product	Salesperson A: J. Doe	Salesperson B: J. Smith	Salesperson C: B. Jones	Total
ABC	$100,000	$100,000	$150,000	$350,000
ABC2	$50,000	$70,000	$100,000	$220,000
Total	$150,000	$170,000	$250,000	$570,000

Sales Operations and Facilities

Your sales management and selling plans should focus purely on the marketing and selling of products. However, the issue of operating the physical locations where inventory is stored or produced, or where sales occur, needs to be resolved as well. For example, if you market your products through a chain of company-owned stores or branches, you need to determine who will operate those facilities. This issue usually falls outside of marketing's parameters in terms of responsibility and budget. Your marketing and sales plans need to account only for how this aspect of your business will be managed.

Sales and Selling Relationships

Selling a product to a customer cannot be done in a vacuum. Sales management and selling are dependent on other marketing mix areas and departments. The product plan, pricing plan, distribution plan, and communication plans must all interface. In addition, sales relies heavily on customer service and production.

Customer service and feedback to product sales are crucial. Your sales management and selling plans must use a tracking and reporting system that includes customer satisfaction measurement (through marketing research), as well as the previously described sales tracking. Customer views in terms of service, product ideas, product changes, product quality, or marketing changes may all have a bearing on current and future sales opportunities.

Advertising Plan

Everyone loves the communications side of the marketing plan because it is perceived as glamorous. Although you have more latitude with advertising, it should be well structured with clearly defined goals and creative parameters. There are three parts to the communications side of marketing: advertising, promotion, and public relations. If sales is the "push," then communications is the "pull." Advertising transmits your marketing message via several vehicles (media) to your target audience (customers). It allows you to alert potential customers to your product's features and benefits so they will want to make a purchase. Advertising enhances and supports your sales and distribution plans. Your advertising options will differ based on your industry (consumer package product, business-to-business/industrial manufacturing, or service).

The process of advertising begins with establishing what message you want to communicate to your target audience. Then you must establish limits and direction for the creative talents who prepare your advertising. Next you need to schedule production and check for any possible legal repercussions. Then you are ready to formulate your media strategy. This means you must select the best (one or combined) mediums to communicate your message. Finally, you will determine the cost of the media purchase and make the placement.

Advertising Expectations and Budgeting

The term *integrated communications* means marketing communication tactics that use all the communication tools together for a common cause, like the term *integrated marketing* means marketing tactics that use all marketing tools together for a common cause. Thus, for an effective advertising plan, your objectives should reflect not only your advertising needs, but your total marketing and communication needs. Your objectives should reflect your desire to produce a product-customer-oriented marketing campaign that generates sales directly or through your sales and distribution channels.

Many of your goals will be driven by the product life cycle, customer life cycle, and market life cycle models, which can provide a basis for tactical plans. In planning your advertising objectives, ask yourself the following questions:

- What are you trying to achieve through advertising?

- Whom do you want to reach?

- When do you want to reach them? (timing and time span)

- Where should you reach them? (geographic coverage)

- How often should you reach them? (frequency)

- What mediums will you use?

Your objectives should reflect the answers to these questions and your marketing process, as well as the level of technology you will be using. This technology can be in the form of sales and delivery automation systems and/or marketing connections used (e.g., the Internet). Use Format 39 to record your advertising objectives.

Format 39

Advertising Plan

20*00*

Product	Objectives	Expected Results
ABC	*Maintain reach and frequency levels with existing ads*	*Continue to saturate market with traditional message*
ABC2	*Same*	*Same*
Overall product line	*Utilize the most effective advertising strategy*	*Maintain solid advertising awareness of products to continue stable sales*

Your advertising budget will focus on creation, production, and media placement (fees and time) activities. It will also represent your integrated marketing approach. Therefore, your budget dollars will be shared between your communication efforts. Format 40 provides a method of establishing what you will spend on advertising over the coming year. In addition, you may want to note how you plan to pay your advertising bills. Will you use a straight payment, shared payment, or exchange/trade?

Format 40

				2000
Product	Activity	Cost ($)	Percentage of Sales	
ABC	Media placement only	20,000	2.0	
ABC2	Creative/media	20,000	2.0	
Total		40,000	4.0	

Identifying Your Advertising Message

There are many parts to marketing management using advertising. One part is to define who is most likely to be a customer (customer profiling) and then match those profiles to actual names and locations of potential customers. Another part is determining what type of message you will be sending to those customers to influence them to purchase your products. In the consumer package product industry, the advertising message is extremely important; many times it is the only thing a prospective customer can go by in deciding to buy your products. Also in this industry, the product's message must draw attention to the product and tell shoppers why they need it.

Your advertising message acts as your primary tactical tool. Along with your medium/media selection and placement, your advertising tactics will concentrate on the following goals:

- Establishing awareness of the product by informing, persuading, reminding, or improving attitudes toward the product

- Reaffirming the importance of your product

Format 41 provides a method of establishing what type of message you will communicate to your customers.

Planning Creative Development

In marketing management, advertising must be used in a controlled fashion. Creativity must be functional first and interesting second. In consumer package product marketing, every communication device must be designed to sell the product. Format 42 provides a method of establishing what type of creative plan you will use to reach your audience. Consider elements such as design, copy, audio, and video.

Format 41

Product	Message	Expected Results
ABC	Inform (awareness)	Continue to establish product availability and benefits
ABC2	Remind (awareness)	Reinforce customer perception of product capabilities
Overall product line	Continue to promote products through awareness	Maintain customer interest by providing information regarding product value and customer support

Format 42

Product	Creative	Expected Results
ABC	No creative work planned	Continued use of old ads
ABC2	Same	Same
Overall product line	Use old creative elements, handle through in-house art department	Make ads meet needs of customers

Planning Final Advertising Production

Once the advertising creative concept has been developed, it must move into production. Artwork must be produced and prepared for reproduction. The various stages of production (such as layout and design, typesetting, mechanicals, and printing) must be scheduled and the quality of the work must be monitored. Format 43 provides a method of determining how you will handle your final production activities.

Format 43

Product	Production	Expected Results
ABC	No change	Continue with same ads
ABC2	Same	Same
Overall product line		Stabilize ads' image/theme

Avoiding Legal Problems

In marketing today, legal exposure is a tremendous issue. This is true in the case of advertising creative work. It is highly recommended that you retain legal counsel to advise you on these issues. You can, however, go a long way in assisting your attorneys and yourself by assessing your exposure levels regarding your creative and final production work in the following key areas:

- Advertising claim substantiation

- Unfair or deceptive messages

- Location of registered trademarks

- Guarantees or testimonials

- Use of rereleased images

- Proper labeling (e.g., Surgeon General warnings)

Format 44 provides a method of identifying any legal concerns you might have and what resulting actions you might take.

Format 44		
Product	**Control**	**Expected Results**
ABC	No change	No problems
ABC2	Same	Same
Overall product line	Little or no change	Small legal review to protect interests

Planning Medium Selection

Of all the marketing mix functions, nowhere do you have more important options than in selecting advertising media. Once you have selected the right message and established the most effective method of reaching your customer with that message, you must select one medium or several to use. When selecting your media, you must consider whether you will be penetrating the market locally, regionally, or nationally. Your choice must be cost-effective and have high impact; in short, it must meet your advertising objectives. In selecting the proper media to use, you should first establish criteria for your choice and then do some limited testing of possible media. The consumer package product industry uses media that reach customers by where they shop, where they live, their mode of travel, how they obtain information, and where they work.

Direct marketing/response has become a hot area, especially using database marketing and MIS lead-generation programs. It is cost-effective and completely trackable and can reach highly selected customers. Standard mass marketing techniques such as broadcast or network television, in contrast, are very expensive and difficult to track, and they cannot be delivered to small customer groups. Another trend is using mixed media and integrated marketing communication techniques. Advertising messages may be transmitted by the media listed in Exhibit 3-3. Format 45 provides a method of identifying which media you will use.

Exhibit 3-3

Media Options

Mediums	Media
Electronic/mass marketing	
	• TV (broadcast)—spot commercials, tag line, on-screen readout
	• TV (cable)—spot commercials, tag line, on-screen readout
	• Radio
	• Motion picture insert
	• Motion picture (videocassette insert)
Direct marketing/response (interactive)	
	• Direct mail—solo (invitation to inquire, preapproval)
	• Direct mail—co-op
	• Telemarketing (outbound)
	• Telemarketing (1-800/1-888/1-900)
	• PC/Internet and intranet
	• Cable TV
	• Direct satellite
	• Catalogs and on-line shopping
	• Voice mail
	• CD-ROM
	• CD-ROM on-line services
	• Digital video disk and videocassette
	• Fax
	• Pagers
	• Point-of-marketing video connect (in-store kiosks)

continued

Exhibit 3-3 *(continued)*

Media Options

Mediums	Media
Outdoor/general signage	
	• Billboard
	• Transit
	• Window/door signs in stores
	• Point-of-purchase (POP) displays—floor displays/stands, coupon dispensers, video grocery carts, shelf-talkers/danglers, counter/shelf units, testers/sampling devices ("in-store marketing")
Sports marketing	
	• Individual personalities
	• Event and/or sport series
	• Teams
	• Facilities (e.g., arena)
Print	
	• Newspaper
	• Freestanding insert
	• Brochure/support insert
	• Internal imaging—corporate logos, letterhead, envelopes, business cards
	• Magazine
	• Yellow pages
	• Directories
	• Event programs
Specialty	
	• Posters
	• Sales premiums (to customers)
	• Slide cards/counter cards
	• Shopping bags
	• Banners
	• Apparel and merchandise
	• Prepaid long-distance phone cards
	• Digital coupons and checks
	• Virtual reality arcade machines
	• Flyers and door hangers

Format 45		
Product	**Medium**	**Expected Results**
ABC	Continue print ads	Maintain advertising campaign and communicate product superiority to customer
ABC2	Same	Same
Overall product line	Balanced mix	Keep current customers and obtain new ones

Planning Media Vehicle Selection

While the *medium* is the type of vehicle you use, such as television or print, the *media vehicle* is the actual physical or broadcast device by which you transmit your advertising message. *USA Today*, for example, is a media vehicle in the print medium.

In this section you will consider the media vehicle to determine the best way to reach your target audience for the least cost. In the consumer package product industry, this is a crucial factor because of how difficult it is to reach a customer. Consumers are heavily bombarded with information. As a result, you must devise a plan of attack that can get through to consumers and persuade them to buy your product. Most media placement processes are based on the following factors:

- Media factors, including gross rating points (GRP), a measure of audience exposure, cost per thousand people reached (reach and frequency), and cost per sale

- Media demographics relative to prospects

- Media characteristics relative to creative requirements

- Media availability

- Media costs ("bang for the buck")

If you are placing media regionally or nationally rather than locally, or you are placing ads in radio, TV, and national publications, you should obtain media buying services.

Format 46, on the following page, provides a method of establishing how you will place your media.

Format 46		
Product	**Media**	**Expected Results**
ABC	*Media placed by GRP*	*Same strong results as last year, but slightly improved*
ABC2	*Placed by availability*	*Quick coverage, hitting target audience, establishing product*
Overall product line	*Use a mix of placement methods*	*Continue to establish products by mixing media and exposures*

Medium/Media Selection and Sales Systems

In selecting how you wish to transmit or communicate your message and therefore influence customers to buy your product, you need to consider many issues. You need to determine how much of a role technology (in terms of automated selling systems) will play in your overall marketing efforts. If your approach is to use these new technologies in some sort of mixture with traditional advertising and/or traditional marketing/sales tactics, your advertising plans need to reflect this approach. Your marketing mix function (in this case, advertising) will reflect an integrated quality that complements the marketing actions available.

The following issues are what you need to consider in developing your medium/media selection criteria:

- Integration of advertising mix (individual use and grouping of mediums and media)

- Integration of communication mix (advertising, promotions, and public relations)

- Integration of marketing mix (all marketing functions)

- Integration of other departments

- Integration of other companies/divisions (co-op/joint ventures/cross promotions)

Lead Processing and Management

With your advertising medium/media selected, the goal is to alert and prompt a customer to inquire about and purchase the product you are offering. The inquiry aspect acts as the response to the advertising, perhaps in the form of a customer visiting a place of business and placing an order. In the modern world of marketing, you want the response to be in the form of a physical record of the customer inquiry, known as a lead.

Lead processing and management needs to be included as an element of your marketing plan. It typically appears in your advertising and/or promotion plans because the catalyst for a lead being generated normally comes from a communication effort. Even those leads that come from sales or other forms of marketing need to be handled as part of your advertising program.

Lead processing and management is defined as the mechanism to produce, record, and direct a lead into a structure that categorizes that lead by product, customer, market, marketing channel or system, sales territory/salesperson, and/or retail location. The lead is tracked using a coding system and monitored for success. The results drive future marketing and lead-generation plans. Your tracking needs to measure the effectiveness of your leads, which includes assigning a "status" to each. Status may be labeled in the following ways:

- Active or inactive

- Close/sale or turndown

- Referral, unsolicited, or solicited

- Customer type (new, current, or former)

The bottom line is the value of the lead. This can be measured in many ways, but typically a lead is measured by three methods:

- Cost per lead

- Cost per response

- Cost per sale (from lead)

These three methods will tell you how one successful lead type is different from another. Of course, lead-to-sale performances are based on many factors, such as sales acceptance (the salesperson's willingness to work the lead) or customer acceptance (the customer's willingness to respond). The key is to select a medium/media mix that can be tied back to a lead, then to develop a process to accept and distribute these leads quickly. Again, depending on the level of technology being employed in your marketing plans, the lead will play different roles. The introduction of an automated sales system will include lead generation as a centerpiece of marketing performance.

Support Resource Management

In forming your advertising plans, you need to account for the relationships on which you will depend to deliver your marketing goals on time and on budget. We have already discussed integration issues that profiled the parties you need to include in your advertising plans. In addition, however, you need to include any external vendors that may be supplying you with services. This can include medium/media placement and buying services. Even the most complete marketing department will contract with some outside agency to provide a service. Your budget and advertising plans need to reflect this aspect of your business affairs.

Tracking Advertising Response

You should employ some type of advertising tracking plan to follow the effectiveness of your advertising plans. You should monitor not only the number of responses, but the effect the medium and message selected had on the purchase of your products.

We have discussed the aspect of lead management and the measurement of lead value on your sales efforts. This applies to all forms of mediums/media you select. Although some mediums/media are easier to track than others, the concept remains the same: you must track advertising effectiveness. In measuring the performance of your advertising, you'll need to consider all the dynamics that go into an effective advertising plan. You will need to address the creative, production, message, and/or media placement (when, against what, on which channel, on what show, etc.). You will need to look at not just the number of customers who responded and made a purchase (frequency and volume), but also why and for how much.

Format 47 provides a method of determining what type of advertising tracking you plan to perform throughout the coming year.

Format 47		
Product	**Tracking**	**Expected Results**
ABC	Lead generation tracking of ads in magazines	Document response and determine its productivity
ABC2	Same	Same
Overall product line	Media effectiveness tracking of TV ads to sales activity	Same

Promotions Plan

Promotion is the second part of the marketing communications equation. The purpose of promotions is to support and enhance your advertising strategies. Promotion is described as any marketing events, special value-added programs, or giveaway or sale of secondary products designed to increase sales of your primary products. Once promotions was considered just an "extra" way to promote your products. Today it has a major impact on product sales. Sales promotions in this context do not include incentives for salespeople to sell more. Promotion uses the same methodology as advertising. The difference lies in the type of mediums. Your promotion options will vary depending on your industry (consumer package product, business-to-business/industrial manufacturing, or service).

Expectations and Budgeting

Your first step in your promotions plan is to establish the results that will contribute to meeting your marketing goals, and how much it will cost to achieve these results. Format 48 provides a method of presenting what you will spend on promotion over the coming year. Costs for promotion activities include creative, final product, and production. In addition, you will need to note how you pay promotion expenses as you did when planning advertising. Many of your goals will be driven by the product, customer, and market life cycle models, which can give you a basis for forming tactical plans.

Format 48			
Promotions Plan			
			20*00*
Product	Activity	Cost ($)	Percentage of Sales
ABC	*Creative, production, final production*	*10,000*	*1.0*
ABC2	*Same*	*10,000*	*1.0*
Total		*20,000*	*2.0*

In setting your promotions objectives, you should ask yourself what you want to achieve; whom you wish to reach; and when, where, how often, and via which media you should reach them. In addition, you need to include the life cycle stage of each of your products to form a baseline for your thoughts. Format 49 provides a method of defining your objectives for the coming year.

Format 49		
Product	**Objectives**	**Expected Results**
ABC	Support advertising efforts by increasing in-state purchase incentives	More visibility and sales
ABC2	Same	Same
Overall product line	Use traditional and new technology	Continue to reach customers and promote sales growth

Identifying Your Promotions Message

Your promotions message should reflect both your promotions objectives and your advertising message and should support and complement your advertising actions. Your promotions message acts as the primary tactical tool for this function. Along with your medium/media selection and placement, your promotional tactics will concentrate on the following goals:

- Establishing awareness of the product by informing, persuading, reminding, or improving attitudes toward the product

- Reaffirming the importance of your product

Use Format 50 to record your message for each product and its expected result.

Format 50		
Product	**Message**	**Expected Results**
ABC	Inform (awareness)	Enhance advertising strategy by maintaining promotions
ABC2	Remind (awareness)	Same
Overall product line	Continue to promote products through awareness	Same

Planning Promotions Creative Development

As in advertising, the creative aspect of promotions must be designed to sell the product and be based on criteria that meet the promotions objectives. Format 51 provides a method of identifying the creative developments you will use in your promotions plan.

Format 51

Product	Creative	Expected Results
ABC	Art, copy, audio, video for trade show booth and POP	Better control over promotional activities
ABC2	Same	Same
Overall product line	Use all creative methods to produce promotional pieces	Same

Planning Final Production of Promotions

Once the creative promotion concept has been developed, it must move into production. The finished artwork must be completed and prepared for reproduction. The stages of production must be scheduled and monitored for quality. In promotions, this may include construction of incentive devices, trade show booths, and displays. Format 52 provides a method of establishing your final production methods.

Format 52

Product	Production	Expected Results
ABC	—	—
ABC2	—	—
Overall product line	Handle and schedule all production work through creative firm	Match advertising image and quality

Avoiding Legal Problems

As in advertising, when planning promotions you must make sure you are not violating anyone's rights. It is highly recommended that you retain the services of legal counsel to advise you on these issues; in the meantime, you can go a long way in assisting your attorneys and yourself by assessing your exposure levels regarding your creative and final production work in the following key areas:

- Substantiation of claims

- Unfair or deceptive messages

- Location of registered trademarks

- Guarantees and testimonials

- Use of rereleased images

Use Format 53 to record any legal concerns associated with your promotions efforts and state what results are expected.

Format 53		
Product	**Control**	**Expected Results**
ABC	*Keep attorneys on retainer to handle any claims*	*Protect by limited exposure*
ABC2	*Same*	*Same*
Overall product line	*Same*	*Same*

Selecting the Medium

Once you have selected the right message and established the most effective method of reaching your customer with that message, you must select one medium or several to use. When selecting your medium, you must consider whether you will be penetrating the market locally, regionally, or nationally. Your choice must be cost-effective and have high impact; in short, it must meet your promotions objectives. The consumer package product industry uses media that reach customers by where they shop, where they live, their mode of travel, how they obtain information, and where they work.

Promotions messages may be transmitted by the mediums and media listed in Exhibit 3-4. Format 54 provides a method to record the mediums/media you will use for your promotions messages.

Exhibit 3-4

Media Options

Mediums	Media
Event promotions	
	• Time period campaigns
	• On-site parties/programs
	• Contests/sweepstakes/games
Sales promotions (customer oriented)	
	• Price specials (discounts, rebates)
	• Product demonstrations/sampling (in-store/at home)
	• Purchase incentives (in-store couponing, trading stamps, premium offers, money-back offers/cash refunds, value-added purchases/ free gifts/bonus packages)
Sponsorship	
	• Sports events
	• Community and charity projects
	• Corporate functions
	• Pop music/entertainment tours
	• Festivals and fairs
	• Arts
Merchandising	
	• Endorsements
	• Licensing of name
Trade shows	
	• Show and booth selection
	• Display/exhibit creation
	• Show and attendee reception management
	• Marketing materials supply
	• Transportation and setup
	• Lodging
	• Lead-generation management

Format 54		
Product	**Medium**	**Expected Results**
ABC	Trade shows, purchase incentives, rebates	Reinforcement of advertising message, image, theme
ABC2	Same	Same
Overall product line	A strong promotional mix for all products	Enhanced advertising impact

Selecting the Media Vehicle

In this section, you consider the media vehicle to determine the best way to reach your target audience for the least cost. In the consumer package product industry, this is a crucial factor because of how difficult it is to reach a customer. Customers are heavily bombarded with information. As a result, you must devise a plan of attack that can get through to potential customers and persuade them to buy your product. Media vehicle choice is based on the vehicle's demographics, creative characteristics, costs, and availability. Use Format 55 to record the media vehicle choices you make for each product and your overall product line.

Format 55		
Product	**Media**	**Expected Results**
ABC	None	—
ABC2	None	—
Overall product line	None	—

Medium/Media Selection and Sales Systems

Like the systems in your advertising plan, those in your promotions plan need the same consideration. In selecting how you wish to manage your marketing mix to transmit or communicate your message—and influence customers to buy your product—you need to consider many issues. You need to determine how much of a role technology (in terms of automated selling systems) will play in your overall marketing efforts. If your approach is to use these new technologies in some sort of mixture with traditional promotion and/or traditional marketing/sales tactics, your promotions plan needs to reflect this approach.

You need to consider the following issues in developing your medium/media selection criteria:

- Integration of promotional mix (individual use and grouping of mediums and media)

- Integration of communication mix (advertising, promotions, and public relations)

- Integration of marketing mix (all marketing functions)

- Integration of other departments

- Integration of other companies/divisions (co-op/joint ventures/cross promotions)

Lead Processing and Management

With your promotions medium/media selected, the goal is the same as that for advertising: alert and prompt a customer to inquire about and purchase the product you are offering. The inquiry aspect acts as the response to the promotion and may be in the form of a customer visiting a store and placing an order. In marketing, you want the response to be a physical record of the customer inquiry, known as a lead.

Lead processing and management needs to be included as an element of your marketing plan. It typically appears in your advertising and/or promotion plans because the catalyst for a lead being generated normally comes from a communication effort. Even those leads that come from sales or other forms of marketing need to be handled as part of your promotional program.

Lead processing and management is defined as the mechanism to produce, record, and direct a lead into a structure that categorizes that lead by product, customer, market, marketing channel or system, sales territory/salesperson, and/or retail location. The lead is tracked using a coding system and monitored for success. The results drive future marketing and lead-generation plans. Your tracking needs to measure the effectiveness of your leads, which includes assigning a status to each. Status may be labeled in the following ways:

- Active or inactive

- Close/sale or turndown

- Referral, unsolicited, or solicited

- Customer type (new, current, or former)

The bottom line is the value of the lead. This can be measured in many ways, but typically a lead is measured by three methods:

- Cost per lead

- Cost per response

- Cost per sale (from lead)

These three methods will tell you how one successful lead type is different from another. Of course, lead-to-sale performances are based on many factors, such as sales acceptance or customer acceptance. The key is to select a medium/media mix that can be tied back to a lead, then to develop a process to accept and distribute these leads quickly. Again, depending on the level of technology being employed in your marketing plans, the lead will play different roles. The introduction of an automated sales system will include lead generation as a centerpiece of marketing performance.

Support Resource Management

In forming your promotions plan, you need to account for the relationships on which you will depend to deliver your marketing goals on time and on budget. We have already discussed integration issues that profiled the parties you need to include in your promotions plan. In addition, however, you need to include any external vendors that may be supplying you with services. This can include exhibit builders or print and fulfillment vendors. Even the most complete marketing department will contract with some outside agency to provide a service. Your budget and promotions plan need to reflect this aspect of your business affairs.

Tracking Promotions Response

You should employ some type of promotions tracking to follow the effectiveness of your promotions plan. You should monitor not only the number of responses, but the effect the medium and message selected had on the purchase of your products.

We have discussed the aspect of lead management and the measurement of lead value on your sales efforts. This applies to all forms of mediums/media you select. Although some mediums/media are easier to track than others, the concept remains the same: you must track promotion effectiveness. In measuring the performance of your promotions, you'll need to consider all the dynamics that go into an effective promotions plan. You will need to address the creative, production, message, and/or media placement (when, against what, on which channel, on what show, etc.). You will need to look at not just the number of customers who responded and made a purchase (frequency and volume), but also why and for how much.

Format 56 provides a method of determining what type of promotions tracking you plan to perform throughout the coming year.

Format 56		
Product	**Tracking**	**Expected Results**
ABC	Track couponing by freestanding inserts, print ads, and point-of-sale distribution	Verify couponing's effect on sales
ABC2	Same	Same
Overall product line	Track couponing to store volume sales	Improve advertising effectiveness

Public Relations Plan

The final part of the communications side of marketing is public relations. This function interfaces with advertising and promotion. It allows you to take advantage of newsworthy events and activities that could promote your business's image.

The process of public relations uses the same methodology as advertising and promotions; the difference comes once again in the medium selection. In addition, special attention should be paid to your policies concerning media relations, your philosophy on community involvement, and your general publicity practices.

Expectations and Budgeting

Although public relations often depends on free publicity, a certain amount of expense is still associated with a good public relations plan. In general, most costs are generated by purchases of print materials and audio or video production. Format 57 provides a method of establishing what you will spend on public relations over the coming year. Costs for public relations include creative, final production, and production. In addition, you will need to note how you will pay your public relations bills—on your own (straight), in cooperation with another company, or by exchange. Complete the format by placing the activity you expect to use in each row, along with the estimated cost of that action and the percentage of sales that cost represents. Many of your goals will be driven by the product, customer, and market life cycle models, which may provide a basis on which to form tactical plans.

In setting public relations objectives, consider what you want to achieve; whom you want to reach; and when, where, how often, and via what media you should reach them. Again, the life cycle stage of your products will help you in forming your public relations approach. Format 58 provides a method of recording your public relations objectives.

Format 57

Public Relations Plan

2000

Product	Activity	Cost ($)	Percentage of Sales
ABC	Creative production, final production	5,000	5.0
ABC2	Same	5,000	5.0
Total		10,000	10.0

Format 58

Product	Objectives	Expected Results
ABC	Support advertising and promotions efforts by selecting targeted PR opportunities	Enhance public opinion of our products and create a more positive image
ABC2	Same	Same
Overall product line	Same	Same

Identifying the Public Relations Message

Your public relations message should reflect both your public relations objectives and your advertising and promotions messages. It also should support and complement your advertising and promotions actions. As in advertising and promotions, the public relations message acts as your primary tactical tool. Along with your medium/media selection and placement, your publicity tactics will concentrate on the following goals:

- Establishing awareness of the product by informing, persuading, reminding, or improving attitudes toward the product
- Reaffirming the importance of your product

Format 59 provides a method of identifying the public relations message you want to convey.

Format 59		
Product	**Message**	**Expected Results**
ABC	*Improve customer attitudes toward product*	*Position products as "green safe"*
ABC2	*Same*	*Same*
Overall product line	*Same*	*Same*

Planning Public Relations Creative Development

As in advertising and promotions, the creative aspect of public relations must be designed to sell the product and be based on criteria that meet the public relations objectives. Use Format 60 to record the public relations development actions you plan for each of your products.

Format 60		
Product	**Creative**	**Expected Results**
ABC	*Concentrate on using copy and video to promote story*	*Clearer, sharper, and more timely publicity*
ABC2	*Same*	*Same*
Overall product line	*Same*	*Same*

Planning Final Production of Public Relations Material

Once the creative concept has been developed, it must move into production. The finished artwork must be completed and prepared for reproduction. The stages of production must be scheduled and monitored for quality. Use Format 61 to establish your final production plans for public relations activities.

Format 61

Product	Production	Expected Results
ABC	Hard copy and video application only; little production needed	Turnkey operation on producing materials
ABC2	Same	Same
Overall product line	PR firm will handle all production activities	Same

Avoiding Legal Problems

As in advertising and promotions, when planning public relations you must make sure you are not violating anyone's rights. It is highly recommended that you retain the services of legal counsel to advise you on these issues; in the meantime, you can go a long way in assisting your attorneys and yourself by assessing your exposure levels regarding your creative and final production work in the following key areas:

- Substantiation of claims

- Unfair or deceptive messages

- Location of registered trademarks

- Guarantees and testimonials

- Use of rereleased images

Use Format 62 to record legal concerns associated with your public relations efforts and establish what results are expected.

Format 62

Product	Control	Expected Results
ABC	None	Maintain current position of all questionable material reviewed by our legal counsel
ABC2	None	Same
Overall product line	None	Same

Selecting the Medium

Once you have selected the right message and established the most effective method of reaching your customer with that message, you must select one medium or several to use. When selecting your medium, you must consider whether you will be penetrating the market locally, regionally, or nationally. Your choice must be cost-effective and have high impact; in short, it must meet your public relations objectives. The consumer package product industry uses media that reach customers by where they shop, where they live, their mode of travel, how they obtain information, and where they work.

Public relations media include the following:

- Press releases

- Seminars/demonstrations

- Open houses

- Annual reports

- Public service announcements (PSAs)

- Articles for publication

- Newsletters

- Books

- Media kits

- Community involvement

Remember, your options will differ depending on your industry (consumer package product, business-to-business/industrial manufacturing, or service). You should spend time and energy cultivating and maintaining good relationships with the media (reporters). Your objective is to establish a means of communication in order to make information immediately available when necessary. Good public relations means positioning your products on the right side of an issue and informing the media about your position.

Use Format 63 to record your medium selection plans by product.

Format 63

Product	Medium	Expected Results
ABC	Press release	Better communication and relationship with customers and media
ABC2	Same, plus seminars	Same
Overall product line	Use a mixture of media and methods	Same

Selecting the Media Vehicle

In this section, you consider the media vehicle to determine the best way to reach your target audience for the least cost. In the consumer package product industry, this is a crucial factor because of how difficult it is to reach a customer. Customers are heavily bombarded with information. As a result, you must devise a plan of attack that can get through to potential customers and persuade them to buy your product. Media vehicle choice is based on the vehicle's demographics, creative characteristics, costs, and availability. Use Format 64 to record the media vehicle(s) you will be using.

Format 64		
Product	**Media**	**Expected Results**
ABC	Use media demographics in advertising	Maintain positive image with customers
ABC2	Same	Same
Overall product line	Match publishing targets with advertising and promotions plans	Same

Medium/Media Selection and Sales Systems

In selecting how you wish to transmit or communicate your message and influence customers to buy your product, you need to consider many issues. You need to determine how much of a role technology (in terms of automated selling systems) will play in your overall marketing efforts. If your approach is to use these new technologies in some sort of mixture with traditional public relations and/or traditional marketing/sales tactics, your public relations plan needs to reflect this approach.

You need to consider the following issues in developing your medium/media selection criteria:

- Integration of public relations mix (individual use and grouping of media)

- Integration of communication mix (advertising, promotions, and public relations)

- Integration of marketing mix (all marketing functions)

- Integration of other departments

- Integration of other companies/divisions (co-op/joint ventures/cross promotions)

Lead Processing and Management

Although public relations is normally not viewed as a primary source of leads, it can and should be viewed as a source for leads. Once your public relations medium/media is selected, the goal is to alert and prompt a customer to inquire about and purchase the product you are offering. The inquiry aspect acts as the response to the public relations effort, perhaps in the form of a customer calling a toll-free number and placing an order. You want the response to be a physical record of the customer inquiry, known as a lead.

Lead processing and management needs to be included as an element of your marketing plan. It typically appears in your public relations, advertising, and/or promotions plans because the catalyst for a lead being generated normally comes from a communication effort. Even those leads that come from sales or other forms of marketing need to be handled as part of your public relations program.

Lead processing and management is defined as the mechanism to produce, record, and direct a lead into a structure that categorizes that lead by product, customer, market, marketing channel or system, sales territory/salesperson, and/or retail location. The lead is tracked using a coding system and monitored for success. The results drive future marketing and lead-generation plans. Your tracking needs to measure the effectiveness of your leads, which includes assigning a status to each lead. Status may be labeled in the following ways:

- Active or inactive

- Close/sale or turndown

- Referral, unsolicited, or solicited

- Customer type (new, current, or former)

The bottom line (even with public relations) is the value of the lead. This can be measured in many ways, but typically a lead is measured by three methods:

- Cost per lead

- Cost per response

- Cost per sale (from lead)

These three methods will tell you how one successful lead type is different from another. Of course, lead-to-sale performances are based on many factors, such as sales acceptance or customer acceptance. The key is to select a medium/media mix that can be tied back to a lead, then to develop a process to accept and distribute these leads quickly. Again, depending on the level of technology being employed in your marketing plans, the lead will play different roles. The introduction of an automated sales system will include lead generation as a centerpiece of marketing performance.

Support Resource Management

In forming your public relations plans, you need to account for the relationships on which you will depend to deliver your marketing goals on time and on budget. We have already discussed integration issues that profiled the parties you need to include in your public relations plans. In addition, however, you need to include any external vendors that may be supplying you with services, for example, outside creative writing services. Even the most complete marketing department will contract with some outside agency to provide a service. Your budget and your public relations plan need to reflect this aspect of your business affairs.

Tracking Public Relations

If possible, you should employ a public relations tracking plan. In conjunction with your marketing research efforts, you should track not only the number of responses but the effect the media and message selected had on the purchase of your products. As stated earlier, some media are easier to track than others. Use Format 65 to record the tracking methods you will employ.

Format 65

Product	Tracking	Expected Results
ABC	None	Monitor situation. If PR problem occurs, research may be conducted
ABC2	None	Same
Overall product line	None	Same

Legal Marketing Plan

The final marketing mix function, which is often overlooked but is nevertheless part of marketing, is the legal aspect. In any business activity, the legal ramifications should always be considered. Changes in federal, state, and local regulations can make your marketing plans ineffective or even illegal. Federal agencies and the justice system, as well as public rights groups, love to target marketing for the ills of society. It is important to make sure you are taking the necessary steps to prevent any legal action from being taken against you. Your legal options may differ depending on your industry (consumer package product, business-to-business/industrial manufacturing, or service).

Expectations and Budgeting

The process of legal marketing planning begins with establishing how you are going to monitor the legal environment to identify any legal action that may affect your marketing activities. Format 66 provides a method of establishing what you will spend on the legal ramifications of your marketing plan over the coming year. Costs for these activities include litigation protection, lobbying, and patent/trademark filing. Complete the format by recording the activity you expect to use with the estimated cost of that action and the percentage of sales that cost represents. Many of your goals will be driven by the product, customer, and market life cycle models, which can provide a basis for forming tactical plans.

Format 66			
Legal Plan			
			2000
Marketing Function	**Activity**	**Gross Cost ($)**	**Percentage of Sales**
ABC	Product liability litigation	30,000	3.0
ABC2	None	0	0.0
Total		30,000	3.0

Once your budget is set, your next step is to record the objectives you are trying to achieve with your legal plans for the coming year. Use Format 67 to record plans such as protection, prevention, and preparation. The life cycle stages of your products may impact the legal position you select.

Format 67		
Product	**Objectives**	**Expected Results**
ABC	Secure and protect ourselves against product liability suits	Lower liability insurance premiums
ABC2	Same	Same
Overall product line	Control market legal actions that could cause problems	Maintain legal team to help us control legal problems

Monitoring of Activities

So far, we have addressed the legal ramifications of the communication content of advertising, promotions, and public relations. Although that is part of the marketing legal situation, other legal areas also need attention. Certain marketing-related activities must be monitored at all times to make sure your products are free of legal problems, both now and in the future.

Your goal is to monitor actions that might be taken against your products or your industry. You want to make sure you are in compliance with or positioned to take advantage of any changing laws. Areas you should monitor include the following:

- Product liability law and liability insurance costs

- Patent and copyright protection

- Legislative lobbying activities

- Contract protection (noncompete agreements)

Use Format 68 to record any legal activities associated with your product.

Format 68		
Product	**Activity**	**Expected Results**
ABC	Monitor product liability activity	Better prediction of legal costs and PR problems
ABC2	Same	Same
Overall product line	Monitor and prepare to control any and all legal activities that impact our products	Protect our interests and legal exposure levels

Adjustments to Marketing Plans

Any change that occurs as a result of legal actions needs to be evaluated. You will need to immediately assess the impact of legal actions on your marketing plans and try to predict future results. Use Format 69 to record any change that may cause you to adjust your marketing plans.

Format 69		
Product	**Adjustments**	**Expected Results**
ABC	None	None
ABC2	None	None
Overall product line	None	None

Obtaining Legal Assistance

Finally, as mentioned before, you should retain legal counsel and/or maintain relationships with political organizations such as associations or lobbies that monitor and influence legal actions which may affect the marketing of your products. Your objective is to be prepared to adjust or control a situation as it arises. Use Format 70 to outline your use of legal counsel for the coming year.

Format 70		
Product	**Assistance**	**Expected Results**
ABC	Use Johnson & Smith attorneys	Control marketing legal activities
ABC2	Same, plus D.C. Lobbying, Inc.	Same
Overall product line	Use both outside professional firms to advise	Same

Implementing Your Marketing Plan

After you have programmed your marketing mix functions, you need to turn your thoughts into actions. Many great marketing plans have failed because the companies didn't carry out the strategies and tactics they developed.

To convert your thoughts into the results you desire, identify the organizational, operational, and logistical limitations and possibilities of your marketing and company structure. Then establish the time line by which the events of your planning will take place to reach your year-end goal. You will need to confirm your advertising media placement plans to support your overall marketing time line.

Turning Tactical Plans into Actions and Results

The secret to meeting your marketing goals is to realize the problems and potential of the structure you must work within. You have people, plans, and processes, financial and physical resources, and systems to deal with in making your marketing plans a reality. It is not enough to have ideas, you need to get buy in from your marketing department and company. They must believe, accept, and endorse your marketing plans.

Organizational and Operational Issues

Your plans have already established the organizational management structure in which your marketing ideas will be implemented. We also have pointed out the importance of the operational aspect (processes, procedures, policies, controls, and corrective actions), which may need to be altered to match your plans. The main thing to consider and emphasize at this point is, assuming your organizational and operational changes will work on paper, you need to obtain an agreement with those who will produce the results.

Your approach to gaining acceptance for the marketing plan is critical. You cannot just drop off the marketing plan or the marketing mix portion of the plan to marketing managers and expect them to follow orders. Although hopefully they have been a part of your marketing auditing, analysis, and planning efforts, they still need to be included in your marketing implementation release.

Your marketing department and the departments in the rest of your company must be prepared to carry out your plans. Depending on your comfort level with the people involved and their distance from you, your style may differ. Assuming they are qualified, properly motivated, reliable, and dependable, current management thinking is to use the following guidelines:

- Macromanage; don't micromanage.

- Decentralize authority; don't control all decision making.

- Report results and offer improvement ideas; don't enter data and walk away.

- Be flexible and open to suggestions, not rigid and closed-minded.

- Accept and thrive on change; don't get angry because your plans must be altered.

Logistical Issues

In addition to your organizational and operational considerations, logistical issues need to be resolved. Logistics is the management of the physical flow of products to the customer. Logistics are viewed differently in each industry. However, logistics typically can include the following elements:

- Customer service

- Marketing mix management

- Financial planning and forecasting

- Production

- Inventory control

- Order processing/fulfillment/shipping

- Delivery/service support

Logistics need to be addressed in the implementation phase of your marketing plan and reviewed to ensure that the flow of business (in marketing or nonmarketing departments) is not interrupted. Therefore, special attention needs to be focused on the following components:

- Qualified personnel

- Organizational structure

- Operational systems

- Processes, procedures, policies, controls, and corrective actions

Your plan needs to be sensitive to changing logistical issues. For example, your marketing plan is built on the assumption that a condition (e.g., new technology) becomes available as expected. Your plan needs to include what you will do if this new technology does become available, is delayed, or does not become available at all.

Remember, the ultimate focus is not on marketing thinking and planning, but on achievement. You must foster relationships with all who touch your marketing plans and ask them to work as a team to make everyone a success.

Scheduling the Marketing Mix

To adequately schedule your marketing plan actions, you need to consider several viewpoints. The normal way a marketing plan is scheduled is by the marketing mix function rather than the other marketing functions. This involves the basic style of displaying your plan, roles and responsibilities, and activities against or referenced to a monthly time line. However, you may want to consider showing your marketing actions in another form and/or a combination of both. Those options include:

- By target market

- By customer and channel

- By product offered

Format 71 shows the functional-based approach. Like all the format suggestions in this book, you are free to modify it to a style that best suits your industry or situation.

Format 71

Marketing Project Schedule

Function	Responsibility	Activities	Jan	Feb	Mar	Apr	May	Jun	Jul	Aug	Sep	Oct	Nov	Dec
Marketing research														
Project/Plan	Responsibility	Activities												
a. Customer satisfaction measurement	A. Wilson	Techniques, methods, instruments, and tabulations		Begin	———	———	———	———	———	Complete				
b. Advertising/media response	A. Wilson	Same							Begin	———	———	———	Complete	
c.														
Product development														
Project/Plan	Responsibility	Activities												
a. Existing product management	B. Jones	Alterations/modifications						Begin	——— Complete					
b. New product development	D. Smith	Product introduction			Begin	——— Complete								
c. Branding/packaging management	B. Jones	New image/appearance					Begin	——— Complete						
Pricing														
Project/Plan	Responsibility	Activities												
a. Formula changes	B. Jones	Cost adjustment				Begin	——— Complete							
b. Price plan changes	B. Jones	Price repositioning					Begin	——— Complete						
c.														

Marketing Project Schedule

Format 71 *(continued)*

Function	Responsibility	Activities	Jan	Feb	Mar	Apr	May	Jun	Jul	Aug	Sep	Oct	Nov	Dec
Distribution														
Project/Plan	Responsibility	Activities												
a. Channel selection	C. Dunn	Open new outlets		Begin	—	—	—	—	—	Complete				
b. Delivery system	C. Dunn	Hire new shippers			Begin/Complete									
c.														
Sales management														
Project/Plan	Responsibility	Activities												
a. Sales force development	F. Fanning	New hires	Begin	—	—	—	—	—	—	—	—	Complete		
b. Sales promotions	F. Fanning	Bonus program						Begin	—	—	Complete			
c. Sales management	F. Fanning	Sales tracking	Begin	—	—	—	—	—	—	—	—	—	—	Complete
Advertising														
Project/Plan	Responsibility	Activities												
a. Creative/production	M. Beesley	Art, video, audio, & copy	Begin	—	—	—	—	—	—	—	—	—	Complete	
b. Medium/media selection	M. Beesley	Placement purchase	Begin	—	—	—	—	—	—	—	—	—	Complete	
c.														

continued

Format 71 (continued)

Marketing Project Schedule

Function	Responsibility	Activities	Jan	Feb	Mar	Apr	May	Jun	Jul	Aug	Sep	Oct	Nov	Dec
Promotions														
Project/Plan	Responsibility	Activities												
a. Creative/production	M. Beesley	Trade show booth			Begin							Complete		
b. Medium/methods	M. Beesley	Sales promotion/ couponing				Begin							Complete	
c.														
Public relations														
Project/Plan	Responsibility	Activities												
a. Press release creation	M. Beesley	Media relations							Begin					Complete
b.														
c.														
Legal														
Project/Plan	Responsibility	Activities												
a. Product liability	R. Callder	Litigation	Begin						Complete					
b. Lobbying	R. Callder and lobbying firm	FTC monitoring				Begin						Complete		
c.														

Media Placement Selection

The placement of your media purchases is very important. Format 72 is shown in five versions to account for the differences in television, radio, newspaper, magazine, and outdoor placement schedules. The primary value of these different versions is the ability to see at a glance where you are placing your advertisements. The formats demonstrate how, when, by whom, where, and why your media is being placed. Costs associated with media placement will be addressed in Unit 5.

Format 72A

Television Proposal

Product: ABC

Message: Reminding customers of special sale

Date Issued: 1-1-00

Day	Time	Program	Seconds	Rating	HH (000)	From/To	Unit Cost	Frequency	Total Cost
Fri	8 P.M.	The Simpsons	30	10.0	500	Jan. only	$5,000	2 million	$20,000

Authorization: S. Carr

Accepted by: M. Beesley

Format 72B

Radio Purchase Order

Client:

Product: ABC

Message: Reminding customers of special sale

Date Issued: 1-1-00

Day	Time	Program	Seconds	From/To	Unit Cost	Frequency	Total Cost
M–F	8 A.M.	News	30	Jan.–Feb.	$500	300,000 per day	$1,500
"	12 P.M.	"	"	"	"	"	"
"	5 P.M.	"	"	"	"	"	"

Authorization: S. Carr

Accepted by: M. Beesley

Format 72C

Magazine Placement Schedule

Product:					Begin Date:			End Date:			Date Approved:				Cost:
Magazine	Jan.	Feb.	March	April	May	June	July	Aug.	Sep.	Oct.	Nov.	Dec.	Total

Name: *ATA Journal*
Circulation: *30,000*
Closing date: *12-1-00*
Publishing frequency: *monthly*
Rate: *3 × 5, $995*
Number of exposures: *70,000*
Contract time: *1 year*

1 *1 page*
2 *reminder*
3 *4-color*
4 *None*
5 *$995*

Total: *$11,940*

Product:					Begin Date:			End Date:			Date Approved:				Cost:
Magazine	Jan.	Feb.	March	April	May	June	July	Aug.	Sep.	Oct.	Nov.	Dec.	Total

Name:
Circulation:
Closing date:
Publishing frequency:
Rate:
Number of exposures:
Contract time:

1
2
3
4
5

Total:

1: Pages
2: Ad type (purpose)
3: Color/B&W
4: Issue/Theme
5: Cost (media placement and/or media placement commissions)

Authorization: *S. Carr*

Accepted by: *M. Beesley*

Format 72D

Newspaper Proposal

Newspaper: *Times*

Product: *ABC to ABC2 (product line)*

Message: *Introduction (reinforcement)*

Issued: *1-1-00*

Day	Type/Day	Ad Size	Gross/Net	Date	Rate	Number of Inserts	Column Inches	Total Cost
M–F	*Morning*	*Full-page*	*$1,500*	*Jan.–March*	*×7*	*1*	*14 × 20*	*$10,500*

Authorization: *S. Carr*

Accepted by: *M. Beesley*

Format 72E

Outdoor Proposal

Product: ABC2

Message: *Inform customers of improvements*

Date Issued: *5-1-00*

Position	Type	Year	Schedule	Unit Cost	No. Times	Total Cost
13th and Main	Billboard	1	Feb.–Sept.	$2,000	100,000	$16,000

Authorization: *S. Carr*

Accepted by: *M. Beesley*

Unit 5

Determining the Marketing Budget

Determining how much it will cost to market your products and services is a key part of marketing planning. The goal of a successful marketing plan is to make more money and/or save more money in marketing. You can talk about marketing strategies and tactics all day long, but at the end of that day, your department needs to deliver on a goal. Although a marketing plan employs innovative and creative thinking, marketing management and the marketing plan are business tools.

Today, more than ever, marketers are being asked to do more with less in terms of dollars spent. The budget portion of the marketing plan needs to reflect the hard costs of generating sales, revenue, and income. To properly profile how marketing will be allocated, this book provides several suggestions:

- Individual marketing (mix) activities expenses

- Overall marketing expenses

- Product/customer-to-marketing expenses (customer and product profitability)

The drivers for marketing costing come from many sources, but certainly the product, customer, and market life cycles all have important roles. Throughout the marketing planning process, costs and budgets have been established. These budgets can be compiled into an overall marketing budget. The figures comparing costs to percentage of sales can be used to check whether your marketing costs are in line with national averages. This may help you determine whether your cost estimates are realistic and efficient.

Once you have completed the compilation of marketing budget data, you may discover that you have exceeded the limits set by upper management. In this situation, you either champion your cause for added dollars or go back through your plan to see where you can cut or reallocate your marketing expenses.

In addition, you will need to separate the cost of marketing (total marketing mix activities) and marketing operational costs (salaries, facilities, etc.). Depending on your industry and your company's definitions regarding marketing costing, your operational expenses may or may not be part of your marketing plan. They may fall under general overhead expenses in the company's pro forma income statements.

Breaking down your expenses is very helpful in understanding how and where marketing dollars are being spent. From a financial point of view, however, your expense allocation and its relationship to the cost of marketing, cost of marketing operations, and sales and revenue inflows (marketing financial structure) need to include financial measurement.

Your marketing actions need to be tied to a financial-based measurement indicator, such as one of the following:

- Return on investment (ROI), for product development costing to income

- Return on assets (ROA), for overall company resources used to income

- Return on equity (ROE), for use of equity financing to income or stock earnings

- Profit margin, for product/sales performance benchmarking

If your company uses the ABC method (activity-based costing) of calculating costs and allocating those costs back to profit centers (products), you will be able to isolate marketing expenses to financial measurement. If your company allocates costs to cost centers, true product profitability will be a subjective call. In either situation, you need to consider how your marketing financial structure will impact your company's financial structure by linking performance to costs.

Individual Marketing Activities (Mix) Expenses

Format 73 lists each marketing function's budget by activity. You should be as detailed as possible and include all marketing-related expenses. In evaluating where your marketing activities stand in terms of cost versus performance, you should assess the budget of each marketing function, as well as your total marketing budget. Depending on where your products are in the product life cycle (determined in your product analysis), the cost of marketing will be higher or lower. The measuring tool you will use is called *percentage of sales*; this means you are establishing what percentage of a sale is devoted to a marketing expense. For example, if your sales are $100,000 and your cost of advertising is $20,000, the percentage of sales for advertising is 20 percent. This calculation can help you determine whether you are spending too much or not enough on your marketing efforts.

The recommended percentages for cost of marketing are outlined in *Auditing Markets, Products, and Marketing Plans* from the AMA Marketing Toolbox series. When evaluating your budgets, do not simply assume that your marketing expenses will fall within these guidelines. This is very dangerous. The purpose of this exercise is to give you a checks-and-balances system. The correct method of evaluating your marketing expenses is to complete each marketing function's budget, then use the percentage of sales calculation to verify that your figures are appropriate.

Format 73

Marketing Plan Budget by Activity

Marketing Research and Data Management

Product	Activity	Cost (Gross)	Percentage of Sales
ABC	Project #1, Customer satisfaction	$10,000	5.0
ABC2	Project #2, Media response	$10,000	5.0
Total		$20,000	10.0

Product Development

Product	Activity	Cost (Gross)	Percentage of Sales
ABC	Maintenance	$10,000	1.5
ABC2	Enhancement	$5,000	0.5
Total		$15,000	2.0

Pricing

Product	Activity	Cost (Gross)	Percentage of Sales
ABC	No changes	$0	0
ABC2	Modify	$0	0
Total		$0	0

continued

Format 73 (continued)

Marketing Plan Budget by Activity

Distribution

Product	Activity	Cost (Gross)	Percentage of Sales
ABC	Continue plan	$10,000	1.0
ABC2	Continue plan	$10,000	1.0
Total		$20,000	2.0

Sales Management

Product	Activity	Cost (Gross)	Percentage of Sales
ABC	Product tracking	$5,000	2.5
ABC2	Product tracking	$5,000	4.5
Total		$10,000	7.0

Advertising

Product	Activity	Cost (Gross)	Percentage of Sales
ABC	Media placement	$20,000	2.0
ABC2	Media placement	$20,000	2.0
Total		$40,000	4.0

Promotions

Product	Activity	Cost (Gross)	Percentage of Sales
ABC	Creative/production	$10,000	1.0
ABC2	Creative/production	$10,000	1.0
Total		$20,000	2.0

Format 73 (continued)

Marketing Plan Budget by Activity

Public Relations

Product	Activity	Cost (Gross)	Percentage of Sales
ABC	Creative/production	$5,000	5.0
ABC2	Creative/production	$5,000	5.0
Total		$10,000	10.0

Legal

Product	Activity	Cost (Gross)	Percentage of Sales
ABC	Product liability	$30,000	3.0
ABC2	None	0	0
Total		$30,000	3.0
Overall Total		$165,000	40.0

Overall Marketing Mix Expenses

Once you have completed budgets for the individual marketing functions, you should merge these expenses with any other costs associated with the marketing process. For example, you may need to install a computer system or some other type of equipment to work through marketing production. Use Format 74 to total all overall marketing function expenses with operational expenses. Remember that this budget does not include compensation for salespeople, agents, or distributors. That money falls under the function of payroll and should be the responsibility of your accountant or controller. This is known as "operational expenses."

Format 74

Marketing Plan Budget by Overall Marketing Function

Marketing function	$	Percentage of Sales
Marketing research	20,000	10.0
Product development	15,000	2.0
Pricing	0	0
Distribution	20,000	2.0
Sales management	10,000	7.0
Advertising	40,000	4.0
Promotions	20,000	2.0
Public relations	10,000	10.0
Legal	30,000	3.0
Total	165,000	40.0
Operational expenses	150,000	—
Overall total	315,000	—

Product/Customer to Marketing Expenses

Another way to examine your marketing costs is to compare your overall budgets with those for individual products and customer types. Your objective here is to view how much you are spending on a product's marketing plan to specific customers. Use Format 75 to record this information.

Format 75

Marketing Function and Customer Type for Product ABC

Function	Customer A		Customer B		Customer C		Total Market	
	$	Percentage of Sales	$	Percentage of Sales	$	Percentage of Sales	$	Percentage of Sales
Marketing research	10,000	5.0	10,000	5.0	0	0	20,000	10.0
Product development	10,000	1.5	5,000	.5	20,000	2.5	35,000	4.5
Pricing	0	0	0	0	0	0	0	0
Distribution	10,000	1.0	10,000	1.0	8,000	.8	28,000	2.8
Sales management	5,000	2.5	5,000	4.5	6,000	2.6	16,000	9.6
Advertising	20,000	2.0	20,000	2.0	50,000	5.0	90,000	9.0
Promotions	10,000	1.0	10,000	1.0	30,000	3.0	50,000	5.0
Public relations	5,000	5.0	5,000	5.0	10,000	10.0	20,000	20.0
Legal	30,000	3.0	0	0	30,000	7.0	60,000	10.0
Total	100,000	21.0	65,000	19.0	154,000	30.9	319,000	70.9
Operational expenses	50,000	—	50,000	—	50,000	—	150,000	—
Grand total	150,000	—	115,000	—	204,000	—	469,000	—

Product and customer profitability are key indicators of how your marketing financial structure is performing. Traditionally, the focus was on product profitability alone, but in today's marketing world customer profitability is of equal or greater importance. Customer profitability reflects the ability to understand which customer types (profile and status) cost the least to reach and obtain, and which generate the most income. Therefore, customer profitability allows you to pursue the most attractive customers and ignore redirect to those customers who cost more than they're worth.

This approach is an acceptable method of doing business, unless you are regulated by corporate, federal, state, or local laws that prevent you from managing your customers in such a manner. Assuming this is not the case, customer profitability and its relationship with product profitability will aid you in restating how effective your marketing financial structure is at generating business.

6 Instituting Marketing Controls

Throughout your marketing and marketing mix plans, tracking, monitoring, and reporting are always a focus. This is because no plan is perfect and you need a method of watching over the implementation of all your marketing plans. In addition, contingency plans need to be ready in case your plans fail to meet the expectations and budgeting goals established. You need to create marketing procedures and monitor and measure the effectiveness of your plans. This will allow you to make adjustments based on changes in the marketplace. No matter how well planned your marketing tactics are, marketplace variables, new information, government regulations, and other factors can force you to alter your course.

The process of marketing control begins with establishing marketing management tracking procedures. You will then design checkpoints to use in adjusting your thinking.

Reporting and Tracking

The primary tools a marketer has available to monitor the marketing plan's performance are sales reports, marketing and media statements, and ongoing marketing audits. Use the formats in this unit for your reference. You will not include them in your completed marketing plan. They can be kept on file or issued to the appropriate departments.

Cost of Sales/Selling

Sales reporting can be as detailed and diverse as you want. You can track sales by customer, distributor, geographic area, and so on. In addition to sales reporting, you can monitor order processing, inventory, and shipping. Format 76 shows tracking by salesperson and product.

Format 76

Product Sales Report by Salesperson

| | | Product | | | | | | | |
| | | ABC | | ABC2 | | ABC22 | | Total | |
Salesperson	Units	$	Units	$	Units	$		Units	$
B. Smith	100	1,000	10	100				320	5,000
F. Jones	50	500							
S. Carr	50	500							
Total	200	2,000						890	19,000

Cost of Marketing

The other side of generating sales and revenue is spending money on the marketing resources to generate that income. In this exercise, your goal is to monitor your monthly marketing expenditures. Format 77 provides you with a method for checking this activity.

Format 77

Cost of Marketing

Function	Product	Activity	Cost ($)
Marketing research	ABC	Postage (mail survey)	300
Advertising	ABC2	Art supplied (creative)	100
Total			400

Corrective Actions and Managing Change

Once your reporting and tracking procedures are in place, your marketing plan needs to include your ability to adjust to change. As you track and monitor your marketing management performance, you need to be able to make adjustments to your plan, alter or change strategies, and prepare for next year.

Marketing Controls

The first place from which changes could come is the marketing research function. For example, results of a customer satisfaction study may make you change how a product is offered. The second area in which change can occur is the business function of marketing. Changes can develop as a result of a market change, product change, and/or marketing management change. Your goal is to employ a method of tracking these changes and prepare yourself to adjust to them.

The term *marketing controls and corrective actions* means the method of ensuring your marketing plans stay on track and meet the goals they were designed to capture. Marketing controls involve reporting and measuring against a predetermined acceptable benchmark. If a product has a planned sales volume mark to reach or a quality control standard to maintain, reporting will alert you to a product meeting, not meeting, or exceeding this acceptable threshold. If it is not meeting the threshold, corrective actions need to be employed.

Corrective actions are the penalty and program that will be put in place in an area, for a manager, and/or for staff to meet the defined threshold. The penalty is usually some kind of compensation or human resource standard. The program focuses on what actions need to be taken to stop the problem from occurring, to prevent it from recurring in the future, and to get back to an acceptable level of managing the business. In the event that alternative plans need to be employed, controls and corrective actions will alert you to the need for such alternatives.

Contingency Plans

Once you determine what (if any) changes must be made to your current marketing tactics, you'll need to alter your marketing plan. You must have alternative marketing plans and new plans of action in place. These plans can be formal (another marketing plan) or informal (basic thoughts). In the majority of marketing departments today, contingency plans tend to be on the informal side. The goal is to hold sufficient information and/or resource redeployment authority to quickly alter your marketing plan's direction.

Updating and Planning for Next Year

The final control procedure you should have in place is a schedule for your next marketing plan. Even if your marketing planning for the current year is flawless, you need to ready yourself for next year's plan. The result is that you begin to develop your ideas and establish the various programs that will allow you to improve next year.

Your marketing plan needs to include some mention of how you will always strive to improve from year to year. You also need to provide a brief schedule (dates only) to begin the cycle of marketing thinking and planning for the following year.

Unit 7

Presenting the Marketing Plan

You have just learned what comprises a marketing plan and how each component of the marketing plan needs to be assembled and arranged. This unit goes beyond the contents of your marketing plan. Its role is to provide ideas on how to best present your plan.

As stated in the introduction to this book, how you organize and build your marketing plan is different from how you present it. The units in this book took you through the components based on the sequential order of where each component should be placed. At the same time, it discussed how each component needs to be created in relationship to the other components in the marketing plan. To review how a marketing plan should be written and displayed, this section is provided to aid you in properly presenting your plan.

Preparing the Presentation

To build a well-accepted marketing plan, you need to begin by planning how to do this and then doing it. You need to establish the time line for development and then work on the visual elements that make up the marketing plan document.

Time Line Management

The routine you normally follow to build, present, receive approval on, and implement a plan begins in June of any calendar year. Typically a company and/or the marketing department of that company meets at some off-site location to brainstorm the direction for the following year(s). From these meetings, projects, goals, requirements, strategies, and/or tactics are established, and the marketing department will receive its marching orders.

The first thing marketing managers do is audit their marketing management approach. This means they determine how well the current marketing plan is working and what changes need to be made to meet the goals set for the coming year. So, by July, they will sit down with their marketing department (sales manager, advertising manager, product manager, etc.) and begin evaluating and thinking through marketing efforts. By August, the marketing mix requirements (efforts needed to meet sales and revenue goals) are fairly well defined.

By late summer, the main structure of the marketing plan needs to be in place, with sales and revenue and the marketing budget defined. Businesses in the consumer package product and service industries tend to want their marketing plans completed, presented, and approved by early fall. Business-to-business/industrial manufacturing companies tend to want their marketing plans completed by October, presented in November, and finalized/approved in early December. In all industries, the marketing plans take effect January 1.

Visual Elements of a Marketing Plan

Although content is what matters in a marketing plan document, how it is packaged can go a long way in selling your plan to the company. The art of designing and developing a marketing plan blends text with graphics to build a story of how marketing will perform in the coming year. The goal is to balance the text and graphics so narrative is broken up and enhanced by pictorial displays.

Exhibit 7-1 demonstrates how a marketing plan document might be presented. The solid lines represent text and the boxes represent graphics. This sample shows you how to arrange the elements of a marketing plan; you can customize the plan to meet your specific needs. The graphic elements included are as follows:

- Diagrams and charts (e.g., bar charts, Gantt charts, process flow charts, etc.)

- Spreadsheets and tables

- Models (e.g., maps)

Other visual techniques might include:

- Use of color versus black and white

- Photography

- Screen captures (from a computer screen)

Exhibit 7-1

Marketing Plan Document Sample

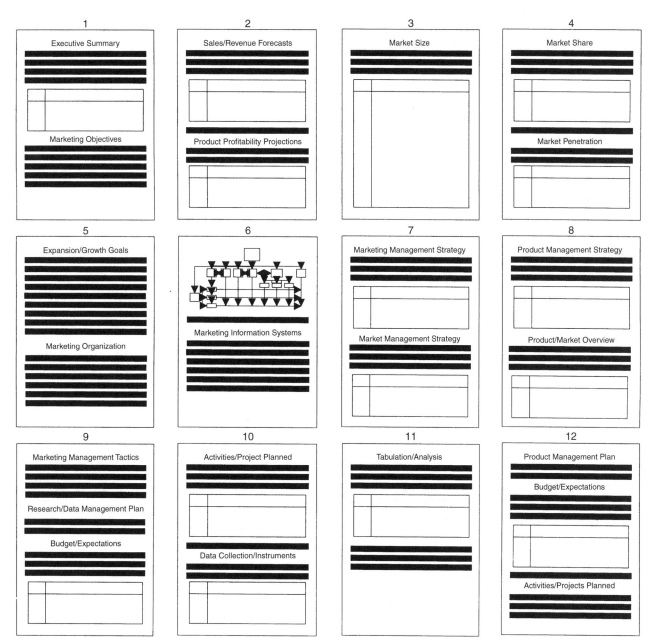

continued

Exhibit 7-1 *(continued)*

Marketing Plan Document Sample

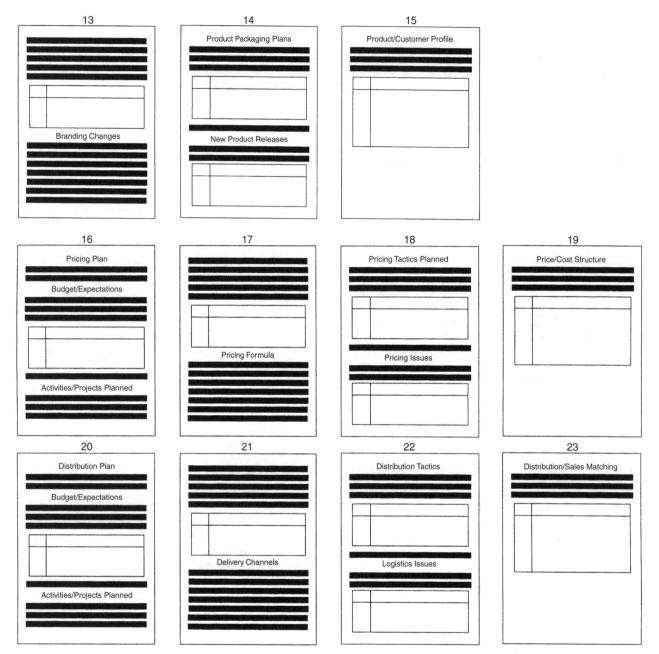

Exhibit 7-1 *(continued)*

Marketing Plan Document Sample

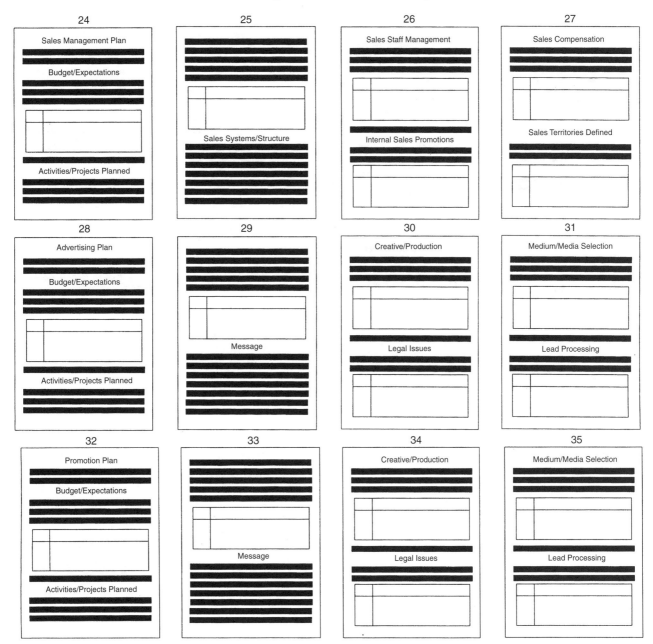

continued

Exhibit 7-1 *(continued)*

Marketing Plan Document Sample

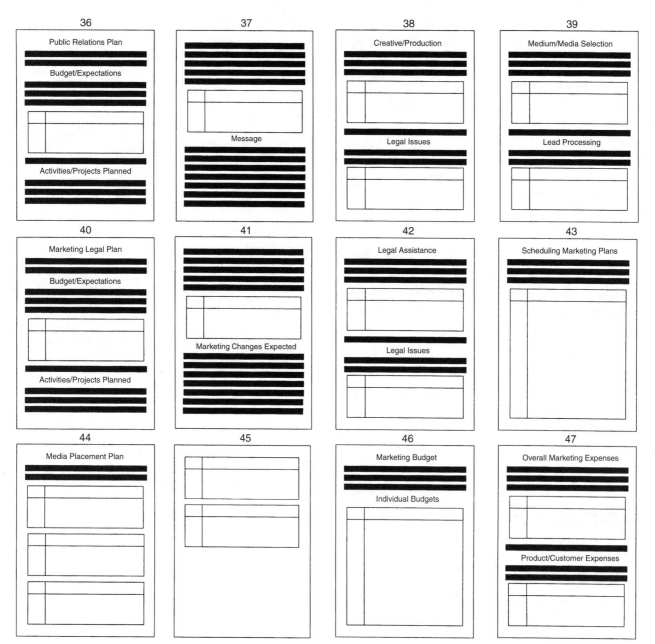

Exhibit 7-1 *(continued)*

Marketing Plan Document Sample

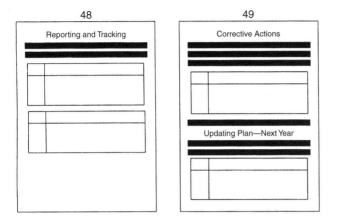

Exhibits and Notations

The marketing plan is a business tool and therefore should only include information that ties directly to your purpose. If you have information that is important to your plan but would serve you better outside of this document, you need to note exhibits. An example of this method would be if you were launching a new product that had a proprietary element. The technical specifications (designed by engineers), which detail the special features of this product, should be used as a separate attachment. From a legal view, this is a prudent move to keep your specifications a secret. From a business view, senior managers will only care how much it will sell in addition to your existing product line and whether it will increase earnings. There is no need to explain how something works, only how well it will serve the company's bottom line.

Presenting and Releasing the Marketing Plan

Once you have built your marketing plan, it is time to present it. As mentioned earlier, a marketing plan is usually developed and presented in sections before a final, full version is officially submitted. Assuming these sections have already been accepted and the final version is now your focus, you need to know how to best present and release it to your organization.

Presentation Outline

The presentation of a marketing plan is of huge significance to a company. A company's primary sales and income will be derived from your marketing actions. As a result, your presentation in terms of content, documentation, and/or visual aids needs to be strong. Depending on the size of your company, its structure, and the industry in which you compete, the marketing plan presentation can be a formal or an informal event. In either case, it should follow these steps:

- Review the executive summary

- Review the overall marketing strategies and tactics

- Review the financials (sales, revenues, and budget)

- Review the key marketing indicators (e.g., market share)

- Review the entire marketing plan, especially the marketing mix plans

- Give conclusions (rereview of the executive summary)

The reality of senior management today is they have limited time. They may or may not allow you enough time to make your pitch. They may control the meeting—hopping around your plan to pick out what they want to know immediately. As a marketing manager, you need to accommodate your managers' needs, while at the same time directing the marketing plan through the sections that establish how you will make the company successful in the coming year.

Once you have presented your marketing plan masterpiece, senior management must accept and approve your plan. It always seems like there are one or two final adjustments that need to be made, but when these changes are done, your plan typically is approved. Your next step is to release your marketing plan to the company.

Marketing Plan Activation

With the help of your marketing department and selected other department managers (finance, production, etc.), you need to have a kick-off meeting or even a party. The purpose of this event is to draw attention to your new marketing plan, the actions you plan to take, and the people, resources, and commitments needed to make the plan a success. After you have released the marketing plan to your organization, you are ready for implementation.

Your marketing plan is a blueprint. It acts as a guide to start you off and lead you through the year. Don't go through the effort of creating and writing a marketing plan and then ignore it! The old saying, "Plan your plan, and work your plan," still works in this modern, high-tech marketing world. Your work is complete for now (in terms of creating your marketing plan), but the real work begins once your plan becomes activated. You need to baby-sit your plan on a daily, weekly, and monthly basis to make sure it is working properly. If the plan needs adjustments (and it usually does), you make the changes, move on, and stay the course.

Beating Your Plan

The reality of a marketing plan is that your assumptions and goals are usually somewhat padded to allow for untimely changes. Of course, the senior management team will try to uncover those cushions, but assuming you can cover your backside, you can make your plan a success the day it is activated. Therefore, your underlying goal is to exceed the expectations you have presented and/or been given.

The focus of your energies becomes the effort to generate more business than planned and spend fewer marketing dollars than planned. By achieving these goals, you win twice. This is especially important if your compensation is tied to your marketing performance.

In the end, your marketing plan needs to be a balanced, business-oriented marketing tool that delivers results. Anything short of this and your marketing plan is ineffective. Marketing management and planning is an inexact science at best, but it can be more exact if you spend the time and the resources to create a marketing plan that supports your company in growth and continued market success.

PART II

DATA REPORTING: FORMATS

Predicting Your Marketing Achievements

Formats 1–5 should be used to help you predict your marketing achievements. See Unit 1 in Part I for explanations and examples of the formats.

Format 1

One-Year Summary of Sales Forecasts

Product	Sales Volume (%)	$	Units	Annual Growth (%)
Total				

Sales Forecasts for One Year, by Month

20___

Product	Jan $	Jan Units	Feb $	Feb Units	Mar $	Mar Units
Total						

Product	Apr $	Apr Units	May $	May Units	Jun $	Jun Units
Total						

Product	Jul $	Jul Units	Aug $	Aug Units	Sep $	Sep Units
Total						

Product	Oct $	Oct Units	Nov $	Nov Units	Dec $	Dec Units
Total						

Product Profitability Projections

20___	
Overall	
Sales in Dollars	
Sales in Units	
Rate of Growth (%)	
Cost of Goods Sold	
Gross Profit	
Gross Margin (%)	
20___	
Product:	
Sales in Dollars	
Sales in Units	
Rate of Growth (%)	
Cost of Goods Sold	
Gross Profit	
Gross Margin (%)	

Format 4

Market Size Model

20___

	$	Units	Annual Growth (%)
Market Potential			
Overall			
Product:			
Product:			
Market Forecast			
Overall			
Product:			
Product:			
Sales Potential			
Overall			
Product:			
Product:			
Sales Forecast			
Overall			
Product:			
Product:			

Format 5

Market Share

20___

	Market Share (Units)	Annual Growth (%)
Overall		
Product:		
Product:		
Product:		
Product:		
Product:		
Product:		
Product:		
Product:		
Product:		
Product:		
Product:		
Product:		
Product:		
Product:		
Product:		
Product:		
Product:		
Product:		

Affirming Your Marketing Direction

Formats 6–8 should be used to help you establish your marketing management strategies for the upcoming year. See Unit 2 in Part I for explanations and examples of the formats.

Format 6

Target Market

Target Market:			
1:		2:	
Descriptors	Counts	Descriptors	Counts

Target Market Strategy

Target Market:				
Customer:	1:	2:	3:	4:

Product Positioning

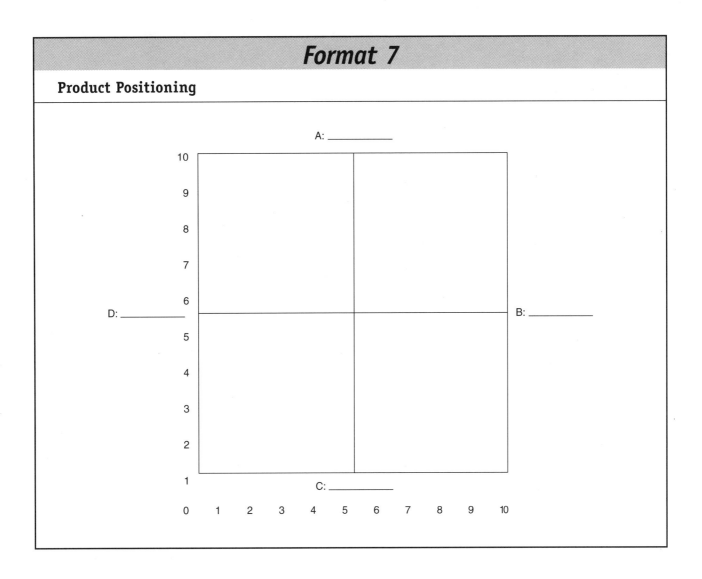

Format 8

Penetration Strategy

Product	Short Term	Long Term

Overall product line

Programming Your Marketing Mix Functions

Formats 9–70 should be used to help you plan marketing activities for the upcoming year in each marketing function area. See Unit 3 in Part I for explanations and examples of the formats.

Format 9

Research and Data Management Plan

OBJECTIVES   20___

Product	Objectives	Expected Results

Overall product line

Format 10

BUDGET   20___

Product	Activity	Cost ($)	Percentage of Sales
Total			

Format 11

PLANNING RESEARCH DESIGN   20___

Product	Type of Research	Expected Results

Overall product line

Format 12

RESEARCH PROJECT DESIGN   20___

Product	Type of Research	Technique

Overall product line

Format 13

DATA COLLECTION AND PROCESSING PLAN   20___

Product	Type of Research	Data Collection and Processing Method
Overall product line		

Format 14

DATA COLLECTION INSTRUMENTS PLAN   20___

Product	Type of Research	Data Collection Instrument

Overall product line

Format 15

TABULATION AND ANALYSIS PLAN 20___

Product	Type of Research	Data Tabulation and Analysis Tools

Overall product line

Product Development Plan

BUDGET   20___

Product	Activity	Cost (Gross)	Percentage of Sales
Total			

Format 17

OBJECTIVES   20____

Product	Objectives	Expected Results

Overall product line

Format 18

EXISTING PRODUCT LINE PLAN

Product	Objectives	Expected Results

Overall product line

Format 19

PRODUCT BRANDING PLAN

Product	Plan	Expected Results

Overall product line

Format 20

NEW PRODUCT PLAN

Product	Plan	Expected Results

Overall product line

Format 21

Pricing Plan

BUDGET   20___

Product	Activity	Cost	Percentage of Sales
Total			

154

Format 22

OBJECTIVES

Product	Objectives	Expected Results

Overall product line

Format 23

PRICING FORMULA DETERMINATION

Product	Pricing Formula	Expected Results

Overall product line

Format 24

PRICE STRATEGY

Product	Plan	Expected Results

Overall product line

Format 25

PRICE/COST STRUCTURING

	Product: _____	Product: _____
Volume (units)		
Price ($)		
Discount* ($)		
Revenue ($)		
Gross Costs ($)		
Gross Profit ($)		
Gross Margin (%)		

*Discounting is based on many factors, such as volume, package features, etc.

Format 26

Distribution Plan

BUDGET   20___

Product	Activity	Cost ($)	Percentage of Sales
Total			

Format 27

OBJECTIVES

20___

Product	Objectives	Expected Results

Overall product line

SELECTION OF DELIVERY CHANNELS

Product	Delivery Channel	Expected Results

Overall product line

Format 29

SELECTION OF DELIVERY CHANNELS

Product	Delivery Channel	Origin of Purchase	Market

Overall product line

DISTRIBUTION PLAN MANAGEMENT

Product	Distribution Plan	Expected Results

Overall product line

Format 31

Sales Management Plan

Product	Objectives	Expected Results

Overall product line

Format 32

BUDGET   20___

Product	Activity	Cost ($)	Percentage of Sales
Total			

Format 33

SALES FORCE DEVELOPMENT PLAN

Product	Plan	Expected Results

Overall product line

INTERNAL SALES PROMOTIONS PLAN

Product	Plan	Expected Results

Overall product line

Format 35

SALESPERSON COMPENSATION AND QUOTA PLAN

Product	Plan	Expected Results

Overall product line

SALES TERRITORY ASSIGNMENT

Salesperson A: Salesperson B:

Product	Expected Results
Overall product line	

Format 37

SALES TACTICS

Product	Tactic	Expected Results

Overall product line

Format 38

SALES ACTIVITY PER SALESPERSON BY DOLLAR AMOUNT

20___

Product	Salesperson A:	Salesperson B:	Salesperson C:	Total
Total				

Format 39

Advertising Plan

OBJECTIVES   20___

Product	Objectives	Expected Results

Overall product line

Format 40

BUDGET   20___

Product	Activity	Cost ($)	Percentage of Sales
Total			

Format 41

MESSAGE IDENTIFICATION

Product	Message	Expected Results

Overall product line

CREATIVE DEVELOPMENT PLAN

Product	Creative	Expected Results

Overall product line

Format 43

ADVERTISING FINAL PRODUCTION PLAN

Product	Production	Expected Results

Overall product line

Format 44

LEGAL RAMIFICATIONS CONTROL

Product	Control	Expected Results

Overall product line

Format 45

MEDIUM SELECTION PLAN

Product	Medium	Expected Results

Overall product line

Format 46

MEDIA VEHICLE SELECTION PLAN

Product	Media	Expected Results

Overall product line

Format 47

ADVERTISING RESPONSE TRACKING PLAN

Product	Tracking	Expected Results

Overall product line

Format 48

Promotions Plan

BUDGET 20___

Product	Activity	Cost ($)	Percentage of Sales
Total			

Format 49

OBJECTIVES

Product	Objectives	Expected Results

Overall product line

Format 50

MESSAGE IDENTIFICATION

Product	Message	Expected Results

Overall product line

Format 51

CREATIVE DEVELOPMENT PLAN

Product	Creative	Expected Results

Overall product line

Format 52

FINAL PRODUCTION PLAN

Product	Production	Expected Results

Overall product line

Format 53

LEGAL RAMIFICATIONS CONTROL

Product	Control	Expected Results

Overall product line

MEDIUM SELECTION PLAN

Product	Medium	Expected Results

Overall product line

Format 55

MEDIA VEHICLE SELECTION PLAN

Product	Media	Expected Results

Overall product line

Format 56

PROMOTIONS RESPONSE TRACKING PLAN

Product	Tracking	Expected Results

Overall product line

Format 57

Public Relations Plan

BUDGET			20___
Product	Activity	Cost ($)	Percentage of Sales
Total			

Format 58

OBJECTIVES

Product	Objectives	Expected Results

Overall product line

Format 59

MESSAGE IDENTIFICATION

Product	Message	Expected Results

Overall product line

CREATIVE DEVELOPMENT PLAN

Product	Creative	Expected Results

Overall product line

Format 61

FINAL PRODUCTION PLAN

Product	Production	Expected Results

Overall product line

Format 62

LEGAL RAMIFICATIONS CONTROL

Product	Control	Expected Results

Overall product line

Format 63

MEDIUM SELECTION PLAN

Product	Medium	Expected Results

Overall product line

Format 64

MEDIA VEHICLE SELECTION PLAN

Product	Media	Expected Results

Overall product line

Format 65

PUBLIC RELATIONS RESPONSE TRACKING PLAN

Product	Tracking	Expected Results

Overall product line

Format 66

Legal Plan

BUDGET 20___

Marketing Function	Activity	Gross Cost ($)	Percentage of Sales
Total			

Format 67

OBJECTIVES

Product	Objectives	Expected Results

Overall product line

MONITORING OF LEGAL ACTIVITIES

Product	Activity	Expected Results

Overall product line

Format 69

ADJUSTMENTS TO MARKETING PLANS

Product	Adjustments	Expected Results

Overall product line

Format 70

LEGAL ASSISTANCE

Product	Assistance	Expected Results

Overall product line

Implementing Your Marketing Plan

Formats 71–72 should be used to help you schedule implementation of your marketing plan. See Unit 4 in Part I for explanations and examples of the formats.

Format 71

Marketing Project Schedule

Function			Jan	Feb	Mar	Apr	May	Jun	Jul	Aug	Sep	Oct	Nov	Dec

Marketing research

Project/Plan   Responsibility   Activities

Product development

Project/Plan   Responsibility   Activities

Pricing

Project/Plan   Responsibility   Activities

Distribution

Project/Plan   Responsibility   Activities

Sales management

Project/Plan   Responsibility   Activities

Advertising

Project/Plan   Responsibility   Activities

Promotions

Project/Plan   Responsibility   Activities

Public relations

Project/Plan   Responsibility   Activities

Legal

Project/Plan   Responsibility   Activities

Television Proposal

Product:

Message:

Date Issued:

Day	Time	Program	Seconds	Rating	HH (000)	From/To	Unit Cost	Frequency	Total Cost

Authorization:

Accepted by:

Format 72B

Radio Purchase Order

Client:

Product:

Message:

Date Issued:

Day	Time	Program	Seconds	From/To	Unit Cost	Frequency	Total Cost

Authorization:

Accepted by:

Format 72C

Magazine Placement Schedule

Product: _____ Begin Date: _____ End Date: _____ Date Approved: _____ Cost: _____

Magazine	Jan.	Feb.	March	April	May	June	July	Aug.	Sep.	Oct.	Nov.	Dec.	Total
Name: _____													
Circulation: _____	1												
Closing date: _____	2												
Publishing frequency: _____	3												
Rate: _____	4												
Number of exposures: _____	5												
Contract time: _____													

Product: _____ Begin Date: _____ End Date: _____ Date Approved: _____ Cost: _____

Magazine	Jan.	Feb.	March	April	May	June	July	Aug.	Sep.	Oct.	Nov.	Dec.	Total
Name: _____													
Circulation: _____	1												
Closing date: _____	2												
Publishing frequency: _____	3												
Rate: _____	4												
Number of exposures: _____	5												
Contract time: _____													

Total: _____

1: Pages
2: Ad type (purpose)
3: Color/B&W
4: Issue/Theme
5: Cost (media placement and/or media placement commissions)

Authorization: _____

Accepted by: _____

Format 72D

Newspaper Proposal

Newspaper: _____

Product: _____

Message: _____

Issued: _____

Day	Type/Day	Ad Size	Gross/Net	Date	Rate	Number of Inserts	Column Inches	Total Cost

Authorization:

Accepted by:

Format 72E

Outdoor Proposal

Product:

Message:

Date Issued:

Position	Type	Year	Schedule	Unit Cost	No. Times	Total Cost

Authorization:

Accepted by:

Determining the Marketing Budget

Formats 73–75 should be used to help you evaluate your marketing budget in each marketing function area. See Unit 5 in Part I for explanations and examples of the formats.

Marketing Plan Budget by Activity

Marketing Research and Data Management

Product	Activity	Cost (Gross)	Percentage of Sales
Total			

Product Development

Product	Activity	Cost (Gross)	Percentage of Sales
Total			

Pricing

Product	Activity	Cost (Gross)	Percentage of Sales
Total			

Distribution

Product	Activity	Cost (Gross)	Percentage of Sales
Total			

Marketing Plan Budget by Activity

Sales Management

Product	Activity	Cost (Gross)	Percentage of Sales
Total			

Advertising

Product	Activity	Cost (Gross)	Percentage of Sales
Total			

Promotions

Product	Activity	Cost (Gross)	Percentage of Sales
Total			

Public Relations

Product	Activity	Cost (Gross)	Percentage of Sales
Total			

continued

Format 73 *(continued)*

Marketing Plan Budget by Activity

Legal

Product	Activity	Cost (Gross)	Percentage of Sales
Total			
Overall Total			

Format 74

Marketing Plan Budget by Overall Marketing Function

Marketing function	$	Percentage of Sales
Marketing research		
Product development		
Pricing		
Distribution		
Sales management		
Advertising		
Promotions		
Public relations		
Legal		
Total		
Operational expenses		
Grand Total		

Format 75

Marketing Function and Customer Type

Function	Customer: $	Customer: Percentage of Sales	Customer: $	Customer: Percentage of Sales	Customer: $	Customer: Percentage of Sales	Total Market $	Total Market Percentage of Sales
Marketing research								
Product development								
Pricing								
Distribution								
Sales management								
Advertising								
Promotions								
Public relations								
Legal								
Total								
Operational expenses								
Grand total								

Instituting Marketing Controls

Formats 76–77 should be used to help you monitor the effectiveness of your marketing activities. See Unit 6 in Part I for explanations and examples of the formats.

Format 76

Product Sales Report by Salesperson

			Product					
	A		B		C		Total	
Salesperson	Units	$	Units	$	Units	$	Units	$
Total								

Format 77

Cost of Marketing

Function	Product	Activity	Cost ($)
Total			

Function	Product	Activity	Cost ($)
Total			

Function	Product	Activity	Cost ($)
Total			

About the Author

David Parmerlee is a senior manager in marketing and product development with USA Group. He worked for Banc One Financial Services for four and a half years, where he directed marketing product management and development efforts. Prior to that he was a marketing consultant for more than ten years. During this period, he helped many types and sizes of businesses sort through the mystery of practicing true marketing management by providing them with solid marketing strategies and tactics.

The strategies and tactics came from his experiences using processes he developed while performing marketing research, analysis, and planning. The processes were designed to produce consistent, low-risk, stable growth and solid results. His books are based on these processes.

His books have sold in the thousands to business leaders, students, educators, entrepreneurs, and marketers all over the world. They are available in three languages. Managers and journalists have touted this marketing planning book as one of the best in the industry.

David Parmerlee's goal is—and will always be—to share information on how to apply real-world and practical marketing, using solid processes, to produce secure marketing results.

The American Marketing Association is the world's largest and most comprehensive professional association of marketers. With over 45,000 members, the AMA has more than 500 chapters throughout North America. The AMA sponsors 25 major conferences per year, covering topics ranging from the latest trends in customer satisfaction measurement to business-to-business and service marketing, attitude research and sales promotion, and publishes nine major marketing publications.

For further information on the American Marketing Association call toll free at 800-AMA-1150.

Or write to:

The American Marketing Association
311 South Wacker Drive
Suite 5800
Chicago, IL 60606-2266
Fax: 800-950-0872
URL: http://www.ama.org